TREASURES OF MEMORIES

TREASURES OF MEMORIES

How Way Leads on to Way

Essays

Arthur T. Vanderbilt II

SERVING HOUSE BOOKS

Treasures of Memory:
How Way Leads on to Way

Copyright © Arthur T. Vanderbilt II

All Rights Reserved

Published by Serving House Books

South Orange, NJ

www.servinghousebooks.com

ISBN: 978-1-947175-58-7

Library of Congress Control Number: 2022937925

Member of The Independent Book Publishers Association

First Serving House Books Edition 2022

Cover Design: Peter Selgin

Cover Photograph: Spencer Kennard

Author Photograph: Lynne Croft

Serving House Books Logo: Barry Lereng Wilmont

To
Joyce Carol Oates
Friend and Muse

Books by Arthur T. Vanderbilt II

Changing Law: A Biography of Arthur T. Vanderbilt

An Introduction to the Study of Law

Jersey Justice: Three Hundred Years of the New Jersey Judiciary

Law School: Briefing for a Legal Education

Treasure Wreck: The Fortunes and Fate of the Pirate Ship Whydah

Fortune's Children: The Fall of the House of Vanderbilt

Golden Days: Memories of a Golden Retriever

New Jersey's Judicial Revolution: A Political Miracle

The Making of a Bestseller: From Author to Reader

Jersey Jurists: Profiles in the Law

Gardening in Eden: Seasons in a Suburban Garden

Best-Kept Boy in the World: The Short Scandalous Life of Denham Fouts

Florham: An American Treasure. (co-author)

The Richest and Most Famous Private Chef in the World: Joseph Donon. (co-author)

The Soul of a House: Adventures in Building an Antique Retirement Account

Olmsted's Vision: The Landscape of Florham. (co-author)

Remaking Florham: From Gilded Age Estate to Campus of Fairleigh Dickinson University. (co-author)

A Slant of Wind: A Summer Afternoon's Reflections on Writing and Publishing

Treasures of Memories: How Way Leads on to Way: Essays

Website: arthurvanderbilt.com

Two roads diverged in a yellow wood,
And sorry I could not travel both
And be one traveler, long I stood
And looked down one as far as I could
To where it bent in the undergrowth;

Then took the other, as just as fair,
And having perhaps the better claim,
Because it was grassy and wanted wear;
Though as for that the passing there
Had worn them really about the same,

And both that morning equally lay
In leaves no step had trodden black.
Oh, I kept the first for another day!
Yet knowing how way leads on to way,
I doubted if I should ever come back.

—from Robert Frost's *The Road Not Taken*

"The distance between past, present and future is only an
illusion, however persistent."

—Albert Einstein

CONTENTS

PREFACE

I'VE ALWAYS BEEN KEENLY AWARE of all the things I simply cannot do.

Anything athletic requiring hand-eye coordination? Forget about it. I experience clean misses in trying to connect with a baseball, a tennis ball, a golf ball, and I mean clean. And the list goes on. Singing? I had my first clue when the principal of our elementary school walked into the auditorium during a rehearsal of our fourth grade Christmas pageant, and, without so much as a word of explanation, summarily plucked me out of the chorus and led me back to the classroom. Drawing? Painting? I'm self aware enough to realize it's just not working. Dancing? Have you ever watched an aardvark give it a whirl? I don't even have anything close to the head of hair apparently necessary to be a social media influencer, or the abs, or, for that matter, everything else necessary to be a model, or soap actor, a television anchor.

From this painfully preliminary, partial listing, it's obvious being in a boy band or a personal trainer, was never in the cards. For most of us, the genetic sweepstakes closes the doors on so many of these fun professions — and verily, on so many careers and possibilities — before we've even submitted our resumes.

Maybe everyone does have some special gift, some talent, though it may be pretty subtle and not so easy to recognize, let alone monetize. It wasn't until rather late in my life that I realized I could remember incidents from my past in vivid, full five-senses detail, and discovered that's not something everyone can do. This talent can certainly be a useful home entertainment system. While seated in a dentist's waiting room, I can turn on a happy memory and replay that distracting tape in my mind, with audio, and change the tape at will. This ability, I came to understand, may well be an essential tool for anyone who wants to write, and may provide an endless supply of material for the writer.

There are times, to be sure, when I wish I had heeded more closely the words of a few wise teachers along the way who urged us to keep notebooks in which to jot down, on a daily basis, ideas, impressions, images from the day. Authors like F. Scott Fitzgerald and Paul Horgan, whose creative notebooks, or parts of them, have been published, have shown us how it can be done, how these jottings can be a trigger to awaken memories and inspire writing. Over the years, at different points in my life, I've started such notebooks, but, to my regret, never kept up this practice. What Allen Ginsberg once called "the long littleness of life" obscures the hidden wonders inherent in every day to such an extent that it seems futile to memorialize the endless gray that seems to shade most days. Too late in life I came to realize that, as Robert Frost told us in his poem "A Peck of Gold", it's actually from deep in these dull mines of gray that the most wonderful shining gems may be plucked:

Dust always blowing about the town,
Except when sea-fog held it down,
And I was one of the children told
Some of the blowing dust was gold.

Without such notebooks, so much of this gold dust is lost forever. I'm sure that as much as I remember, many times more has been lost to the ages, never to be retrieved.

It's curious how the brightest of these gold dust memories seem to be about the smallest, the seemingly most inconsequential moments of our lives. There is no need to follow Hemingway's footsteps to search the world for material. There's no need to plan safaris or trips of adventure and discovery, or follow wars. It's all happening right here, right where we are.

I've always been taken by Thoreau's declaration in *Walden*; "I have travelled a good deal in Concord," he told us. In time, everything in Concord revealed itself to him, just as Emily Dickinson, who lived her entire life in the same house in Amherst, and "never saw a moor" and "never saw the sea," discovered the world was right there: at her doorstep. Having spent her life as a travel writer "wandering the world," Jan Morris found, as she said, that "the truest truths are small ones, to be discovered wherever you are. If I could have my time over again, I think I would choose to roam only my own small patch of country — my bro, as we say in Wales. Instead of exploring continents and empires, I would investigate even more intensely our modest fields, hills and villages; rather than wild beasts of Africa, I would watch the herons on the river, the frogs in the pond." The great British artist, Francis Bacon, once wrote: "When I was younger, I needed extreme subject matter for my paintings. Then, as I got older, I realized I had all the subjects I needed in my own life." For those whose eyes are open, it's all happening here, right outside our windows.

It is these tiny specks of gold from the blowing dust of our lives that can be the most memorable. Way does indeed lead on to way, and there is never time to revisit the wonder of these special moments in our lives — except in memory. The people are gone. The places we knew are gone. Seasons turn. Years rush by. Decades vanish. Schools and exams and applications and colleges, resumes and jobs and time sheets and work shifts and family. Out of the blue — how can it be? — you're bombarded with notices of the upcoming 50th reunion of your high school class, then of your college, then your graduate school. A half century. Looking back, there are entire decades that somehow slipped behind you, decades you can't account for. Where did they go? What were you even doing? Ten year blocks of time: gone forever.

And then, something will remind you: Sunlight swimming on

a carpet as it filters through the blowing leaves of the tree outside your window. The way a fat cloud sails through the blue, windy sky. A face in a passing car. The sound of a voice. A fragment of a song from long ago.

And suddenly, a glimpse of a memory starts to come into focus, until, once again, I'm back. These are not transformational moments. And it may be that they mean nothing. Or maybe everything. Either way, for a few minutes, come join me there.

I

THERE'S A SUMMER PLACE

THE FRAMED PHOTOGRAPH IS STILL where my mother kept it: on top of the dresser in her bedroom where she died. She was a teenager then — in the photograph — seated with her brother in a small wooden catboat out on Barnegat Bay, the year, maybe 1938, when they spent the summer with their Aunt Edith.

Edith was one of my grandfather's maiden sisters, a biology teacher at Summit High School who was so well regarded that she became head of the science department at a time when it was unheard of for a woman to assume such a leadership position ahead of her male counterparts. She rented a floor of an old Victorian house across the street from school, and, during those Depression years, on her teacher's salary, bought for several hundred dollars, a small, very small, plot of land behind the dunes at Normandy Beach along the Jersey shore, and there built a modest summer cottage which became her retreat, her paradise. It was five lots back from the ocean, and an equal number in from Barnegat Bay. Edith built her house not only with a teacher's frugality, but with a science teacher's smarts, elevated a good ten feet above the sand so that any storm surge would pass under it.

From what Edith told us, the ocean beach there, in those early days, was empty, dazzling, pristine, just a few shacks back in the dunes where fishermen would dry their nets and lines and pull up their dories, and a couple summer bungalows, like hers, scattered here and there, all decades before the extension of the Garden State Parkway opened up the Jersey Shore to the masses and led to houses perched side by side on the crest of the dunes, and all the way back to bulkheads built out into the Bay.

Ede would invite groups of her students to come visit on weekends, to enjoy the ocean and her cooking, with some marine biology and seaside botany woven in for good measure. Those were innocent days, days when life was simpler, of ocean swims and sails on the Bay, fish for supper bought right off a boat and blueberries picked in the dunes and tomatoes grown behind her house in the sandy soil she enriched with compost.

The Shore was already changing in the 1950s when we were very young and our parents would take us to visit Aunt Edith after she had retired and was living there all year. It was only an hour and a half drive, door to door, but to a youngster? That was a journey. And as we drove over the bridge across the Raritan River, we left behind the New Jersey of trees and suburbs, of highways, oil refineries, slaughter houses and smokestacks, and a whole new world appeared, of open spaces and big sky, of salt marshes and inlets, of signs for Shore towns with evocative names — Sandy Hook, Long Branch, Asbury Park, Bradley Beach, Belmar, Spring Lake, Manasquan, Point Pleasant Beach, Bay Head, Mantoloking — names that spoke to us of sand and sea and surf, of summer, and, at last: Normandy Beach. We'd turn in on First Avenue.

When we got out of the car in Ede's pebble driveway, we could hear the rhythmic breakers on the other side of the dunes, and smell the freshness of the ocean. Ede knew just what we wanted and would suggest that we hit the beach before lunch. We'd climb the steep stairs in the kitchen to the second floor to put on our bathing suits. There was a guestroom under the eaves, a small bathroom, and what Ede called the "Pilot Room". Through its old windows, you could see over the dunes to a wonderful blue band of ocean, where sometimes a fishing boat would be making its way up the coast. How magical was that view of sea and sky! How that magic is retained in memory, with gentle sea breezes stirring the windows' frail lace curtains, just as in Andrew Wyeth's painting "Wind from the Sea."

I remember the tags she'd give us to pin on our bathing suits.

The stately boom of the breakers as we crested the dunes.

The ocean and beach, as fresh as the first morning.

Lying on beach blankets as Ede described the patterns of the offshore currents, and told us stories of the burning of the *Morre Castle* in September of 1934, just up the coast, the explosion of the *Hindenburg* dirigible in the nearby Pine Barrens in 1937, tales of Barnegat Bay and of the Pines, places which seemed to my sister and me as exotic as foreign lands.

I remember the smell of *Coppertone*, its brown bottle with the Indian on it.

The wonderful warmth of the sand.

Walking back to Ede's house after playing in the surf.

The neighbors talking with her as we proceeded along.

The yellow-white pebbles around her tiny yard.

The exuberant geraniums and "spetunias" in her window boxes which she showed off.

Rinsing the sand off our feet in the enamel basin filled with water she kept at the bottom of the wooden steps up to her house.

Inside, out of the noon sun, all the windows open, the summer breezes stirring the homemade drapes.

Ede set heavy cobalt blue tumblers filled with lemonade at our places around the table in the living room — a wooden picnic table that had been made for her by the shop teacher at the high school. A large oil painting one of her students had painted — of ducks rising from an evening marsh — hung over her fireplace. Above the Bermuda sofa was an oil painting of Normandy Beach at the turn of the century, with a small tractor-like vehicle pulling a dory up from the sea — a scene I asked my mother to describe each time we were there, hoping to hear more stories of when she and her brother, as teenagers, would stay with Ede that summer, just a few years before Pearl Harbor when the world changed, when Don a few years later, at eighteen, enlisted in the Marines and was killed that year in the South Pacific on an aircraft carrier. There was a water color of the dunes that the high school's art teacher had painted en plein aire on a visit, and another, painted by a neighbor, of some fish shacks and a dory in the dunes, paintings that captured the Normandy Beach Ede had known in those early days at the Shore.

I don't think I have a selective memory about this, but all I remember, from all of our visits with Aunt Edith, are sunny, happy days, days of blue skies and summer clouds, of crystal cool water and gentle surf. Because that, back then, was the way it always was when we were very young.

Ede was gone, her house sold after her death, when Hurricane Sandy hit the Jersey Shore in October of 2012. We studied in the newspapers all the aerial photographs of the devastated shore communities, the ocean sweeping right across that narrow barrier beach into the Bay, searched until we found it. There it was. There was her cottage. Still standing amid the chaos. Built for this day she realized was possible.

The paintings of Normandy Beach in the 1930's found their way to our summer place on the Cape, and hung in the master bedroom. When my mother was in her nineties, near the end of her life, tethered to an oxygen tank, confined to a hospital bed in this room which became her world, she would often look at these paintings and recall her summer there when she was a teenager. And say how, someday, she'd like to go back. To see Normandy Beach again.

Such is the lifelong pull of an enchanted summer place.

The photograph of my mother and her brother as teenagers sailing on Barnegat Bay, looking up toward the top of the wooden mast on a long ago summer morning with a spanking sailing breeze, their lives stretching without end before them, sits still on the bureau in that bedroom, a moment in time frozen way back then, a moment that captured it all.

II
CHAPPY

I WAS FOUR, MARJORIE SIX, when our parents must have finally decided they just couldn't' take any more and announced we'd all be going away for the month of July: our first vacation.

They had rented a cottage for the month from good friends in town, whose daughter, Lain, was a friend of my sister's. Lain and her parents would also be there for July in another small house on the same waterfront property which they had inherited from a relative.

Our cottage, our parents explained, was on Martha's Vineyard, an island off the coast of Massachusetts. An island? How do we get to an island? I asked. We'll take a ferry, our father explained, it's about an hour ride. On a steamship. This was already sounding good. Were pirates ever on the island, I asked, and when told there may well have been, it was sounding even better, and better still when our mother added that on the island was a place called Gay Head, which was an Indian reservation. Indians! And even better still when our father opened up on the floor of his den — where my sister and I spent most of our lives with plastic pirates and cowboys and Indians, inventing continuing, increasingly noisy and violent adventures — a road map from the Esso gas station, and traced with a crayon the route we'd be following, until it stopped at water. He pointed out the tiny little island off of Martha's Vineyard where we'd be staying: Chappaquiddick, an Indian word, our parents explained, (an Indian word! By the end of the month, we'd be talking Indian!) that meant: "Separated Island". On the map, it hung off the mainland like the map of Treasure Island we had seen. Is there buried treasure on the island, I asked? There could be, our father answered;

that's the sort of spot the New England pirates might have selected to bury a treasure chest. (He knew just how to preoccupy our thoughts for long stretches.) Will we be able to dig for treasure? Whenever we want, he assured us.

The countdown began, and after an interminable ride in our station wagon before the days of air conditioning, we were at Woods Hole, driving the car into the clanging, banging, echoing, gaping dark bowels of an enormous, mysterious steamship. The whistle sounded. Suddenly, cut free of the wharf, the steamship was in motion, heading across open water: the Vineyard Sound!

Picture the wonderful sensory overload for a four year old from the suburbs. It wasn't long before I found the counter selling captains' hats, and I picked the white one with gold braid and wore it for the rest of that summer. When at last we reached the *On Time*, the little, barge-like two-car ferry for the minute passage across the harbor, from the mainland to Chappaquiddick, I — like Samuel Clemens deciding he would be a river boat captain — had, at the age of four, already settled on my life's work: I would spend my days being the ferry's captain, bringing cars and passengers all day back and forth across beautiful Edgartown harbor.

Our cottage was small, old, unfinished, primitive, the rafters and studs exposed. There was no hot water heater; every Saturday night, our father would fill the tub with water for our weekly bath as he heated on the stove large pots of water, bringing them to a boil, then mixing them in with the bathtub water until it was lukewarm, good enough to bathe us with the strong brown laundry soap to wash away poison ivy oils. The water pump was halfway down the bluff to the beach, in a tiny wooden pump house which contained an ancient contraption that looked like you would need a degree in nuclear physics to start it. The toilet seat was wooden, and our mother complained of getting splinters, and the next summer (yes, of course we returned, we loved it!) carried with her onto the steamship a modern toilet seat, putting it over her head and around her shoulders for a photo op on the deck.

This cottage had been built in the 1920s by a relative of our parents' friends. It had been her caretakers' cottage for the man who looked after her home, a remarkable two-story house that had been built on pilings, from the beach below the bluff out into Katama Bay. There she lived in the summer, out on the water, and ran her antique shop specializing in Spanish antiques collected during her winters in Granada, Spain, which she would sell to the yachtsmen who pulled up alongside. They would sit on the deck around the house and have a glass of sherry with her as they examined her collection. The historic New England Hurricane of 1938 had demolished her home, splintering it to pieces, she had escaped just in time, scrambling up the narrow concrete steps built into the bluff and taking refuge in the cottage. For decades after, shards of porcelain from her collection could be found among the rocks along the shore. The cottage held a few of her Spanish pieces, dark rattan lounge chairs and sofas and tables, but what attracted me most was a yellowing old map of the Vineyard on the wall, with touches like a spouting whale sporting in the Sound.

For a four year old who knew only the suburbs, every sense was alive to everything new: the smell of the scrub pines baking in the hot July noonday sun, the sticky pitch resin oozing through the bark; the sandy rutted road we'd walk every day, down from our cottage to the Vineyard Sound, past Caleb's Pond at the end of Katama Bay, surrounded by that lush wet green marsh with its intoxicating salt water, summer aroma; the soft sand of the beach where we'd encamp with all the gear our poor father had lugged — the green beach umbrella he would open up and the beach towels we'd spread out, and the Scotch Cooler and our rubber float in the shape of a jolly whale; the clear water of the Sound barely lapping sand with the quietest rhythmic swish; friendly summer clouds sailing across wide open sky.

Of course, living on an island, the water, and the boats were everything. From our pine-needled yard, we could look through the branches out over Katama Bay, a protected inlet from the Vineyard Sound which was a perfect anchorage for a fleet of yachts. There were graceful sloops and yawls, forty feet, fifty feet, sixty feet, gleaming white, and one black one (a pirate ship, we were sure, we kept a careful eye on that one each day), all with teak decks and sharp green trim and towering masts, vintage wooden masterpieces before the days of fiberglass and industrial composites.

Despite all of this magnificence anchored at our doorstep, my own aspirations then were very modest indeed: to row a boat. There was a pile of pine logs next to the house which I brought out to the yard and laid in the formation of a rowboat. I would sit in it for hours, in my captain's hat with the gold braid, pretending to row, and my sister and Lain sat in it, too, as passengers or pirates. On any beach we walked, if a derelict rowboat was pulled up on shore, I'd run over and sit in it: Admiral of the Ocean Seas. I presented to our parents a reasonable plan: to take a drawer from the bureau in the bedroom I shared with my sister and turn it into a rowboat. And those days when we happened upon a sandy, sodden ratty length of manilla line almost covered with seaweed, or, once, a mooring can from one of the yachts, were very special days indeed, when I felt we were assembling the component parts of the rowboat that, someday, would be ours.

That's the background for that July afternoon we walked down the steep flight of crumbling concrete steps that had been dug into the bluff, my mother, father, sister, Lain and I, down to the pebbly beach around Katama Bay, a quiet summer afternoon, just a pulse on the Bay, the water hardly licking the shore. I'm sure that afternoon, like all afternoons, I was looking into the water at the black snails, looking at the old wooden dock, twisted and mangled in the Great Hurricane and never restored, the bait fish flashing under its shadows. Lain, Marjorie and I delighted in taking a metal pail and filling it half full of salt water and collecting as many snails as we could, bringing them up to the yard to name and study for several days, before bringing them back to their home in the Bay.

"Sue Santry," my mother suddenly said, breaking the quiet rhythm of the afternoon.

What a strange name for a snail, but OK.

"I think that's Sue Santry," she said to our father, pointing, across the Bay.

She had borrowed her father's field glasses for our vacation and was focusing on a sleek white sloop moored way across Katana Bay.

We didn't pay any attention.

"Who?" our father said.

"Sue Santry," she said, explaining that they had been classmates at Wellesley College, over ten years before.

"I doubt it," our father said. "What would she be doing here? What are the chances?"

My mother remembered that Sue's uncle had a sloop and sailed around New England each summer.

The binoculars passed back and forth, everyone taking a turn and opining on what they saw, or thought they saw.

"It's her," my mother said, giving the binoculars to my father, "I'm sure. Look, right there. Sitting on the deck. Against the mast."

My mother shouted over the water: "Sue! Sue!"

Now we all were excited, and someone suggested we all yell together on the count of three.

One, two, three:

"SUE SANTRY! SUE SANTRY! SUE SANTRY!"

Again and again and again until our words were echoing back from the far shore.

My mother kept looking through the binoculars. She reported that the lady on the deck was moving. She was looking toward us.

We yelled again. Louder still.

Now, on cue, we yelled my mother's maiden name, her college name:

"JEAN WHITE! JEAN WHITE! JEAN WHITE!"

The woman on the deck was waving. She shouted something we couldn't hear.

Our excitement grew, our yelling continued.

A dinghy was being lowered into the water.

She was rowing toward us!

The trim dinghy glided right to our feet where we all had gathered, scrapping onto the shoreline pebbles.

It was Sue!

What were the chances indeed?

Everyone gathered around her, talking about the improbability of it all and getting caught up, from college days to the present. Everyone except me, who was riveted by her handsome dinghy, staring at it, watching it float and move with the tide, being a responsible captain and holding the edge of it so that it wouldn't drift away, giving my eager hands a chance to actually touch it, caress it, dream about it. In fact, I heard nothing of the boring adult conversation until these words: "would you like to come out and see our boat?" I'm sure I was looking at our father with the same expression a dog would have when begging for a juicy treat: I was never sure if being the youngest would preclude me from being allowed to join in on the fun stuff. Blessed Sue indeed meant all of us, and it took two trips to row us out there.

There I was! in a rowboat! Gliding over the water, the sweet, rhythmic sound of oars in oarlocks, drops of water dripping off the wooden blades after each clean sweep, the dinghy snaking around other yachts until we pulled alongside Sue's which towered over us. My father lifted me up from the dinghy and one of the crew reached down and got me under the arms, manhandling me aboard, like a tuna.

This was the sort of improbable event that might start a F. Scott Fitzgerald short story. Was this what life always would be like? I assumed so. It wouldn't, of course. But it was, that one dreamlike afternoon on Chappy.

Maybe it was because we were so young and everything was so new, so different, that other days from those long ago Island summers pop up in memory, decades later.

Our parents had a friend from home who was on the Vineyard while we were there. He was a serious bird spotter and was leading a group on a dawn bird watch. Our parents announced we'd all be going, which precipitated protests: we didn't want to leave our playground around the cottage, didn't want to leave Lain, all we wanted was another wonderful day like today and yesterday and the day before. Interruptions of our cherished agenda? No good. And this would be in Chilmark, across Martha's Vineyard, which would cruelly slice into a precious day. Parents always win such arguments, which, once in a while, I suppose, may be a good thing. After that day spent sneaking through fields and moors, around ponds and swamps and beaches, I was hooked. We began putting out raisins on a bench outside our cottage and soon had daily visits from a friendly catbird. A new world opened for me, and my Life List of birds begun that summer grew for years.

Another day we were wrenched from our sacred routine when our parents visited some friends from New Jersey who were staying in Chilmark. A lost day, until their son, who was in graduate school, studying to become a geologist, made an appearance and took us to the old barn behind their home. Just to see that barn would have been an experience, one of the very early Vineyard barns from over a century before when the landscape was dotted with small farms. He had a workbench along a wall, piled with nondescript rocks. He took one, and, like a magician, said "Watch this." He secured it in a vise, took a geologist hammer, studied the stone and gave it a light tap, splitting it into two parts, which he removed from the vise. And showed us the fossil inside. And described what it was and how many millions of years old it was, and how it was formed and where he had found it. Such was the impact of that afternoon that I questioned whether I really wanted to spend a lifetime captaining the *On Time* ferry, and balanced it against the life of a geologist. I began collecting rocks and minerals, a hobby which lasted until I signed up for a geology course my freshman year in college and dropped out after the first class, realizing that this was not going to be the sort of fun I envisioned that afternoon in an old barn in a field on the Vineyard.

Birds. Rocks and minerals and fossils. The world around me was opening up. And the wider world was coming closer. As we slept peacefully in our cottage that foggy night of July 25, 1956, not so far away the luxury Italian ocean liner, the *Andrea Doria* collided off the coast of Nantucket with the Swedish passenger liner, *Stockholm*, perhaps the worst maritime disaster since the *Titanic*. The *Andrea Doria* took an immediate list as its watertight compartments were breached and flooded, making the lowering of many of its lifeboats impossible. Rescue efforts continued through the night, as we slept, and into the next morning when the ship plunged to the bottom of the sea. It wasn't long before deck chairs, life preservers and other debris were washing up along Chappy's Wasque Beach where we often had enjoyed evening picnics . Every detail of the tragedy filled these summer days, and our imagination.

And then there was the day we tried to outrun a hurricane. It was the end of August, time to leave Chappy, our last day. Our parents had gotten word about Hurricane Carol which had hit hard the southern part of the United States, but was diminishing as it headed up the coast. Until it got sneaky and made some surprise twists and was slamming Connecticut and Rhode Island, with winds of 80-100 mph and gusts over 135 mph, and storm surges at coastal towns of over fourteen feet. I remember the radio in our cottage turned on again and again to get the latest updates, our parents quietly debating between themselves the chances of getting off the Island before it struck, versus our chances of being able to ride it out in the old cottage. And then the die was cast: we would evacuate before dawn.

My sister and I were pulled out of bed around 3:00 a.m. and after a quick breakfast, our father wrapped woolen blankets around us and rushed us through the torrential rain of that wild night into the station wagon which he had packed the night before and parked as close to the cottage as he could get it. We would learn later that ours was the last trip across the channel the *On Time* made that day, and ours the last steamship crossing the Vineyard Sound. Huddled in the car, the wind battling the station wagon, lashing the rain against us, the windshield wipers fighting the good fight, full speed. Going through Taunton, I remember our parents, saying to each other that the water was now over the hubcaps, and, I'm sure, wondering what they had gotten us into and how to get us safely out. On we fought, everyone holding their breath until at last we emerged beyond the hurricane and inhaled.

Again, I assumed that such flights were part of the summer season in New England, and I wish now I had noticed and remembered every detail of that once in a lifetime escape.

A hurricane. The sinking of a luxury liner. An introduction to the natural world of birds and rocks and minerals. All part of our summer on Chappy. But what sticks most vividly in memory are the smallest moments.

In a tiny seaside summer cottage, there are no secrets.

It wasn't long before we learned the reason why, one day, our mother didn't want to do anything and was acting grumpy and irritable: she was "blocked", our father confided to us. And therefore, he told us, we would all be heading over to the pharmacy in Edgartown to get a bottle of Haley's M.O., a magic elixir he said would cure the problem.

It certainly wasn't long before my sister and I had reported all of these confidences to Lain, and the three poet laureates of the Island had composed what would become an immortal couplet:

When things are moving kind of slow?
Take Hayley's M.O.

Wherever one of us recited these classic lines, which was rather quite often, we didn't just smile, we didn't just giggle and laugh. The three of us would be so convulsed that we ceased to function. And it wasn't very long before the continued repeated recitation of this verse in the presence of any grown-up was banned. This, of course, necessitated circumventing such an unreasonable edict, which in short order gave birth to our imaginary character, Connie Constance, and endless discussions of whether Connie had come for a visit, and whether she was currently a guest in the cottage. We would speculate on whether Connie's friend, the Baby Dia, was due for a visit. And heaven forbid, on those rare occasions when we all went out for dinner with Lain's parents at a local café, and someone ordered that New England favorite, Indian Pudding, and the waitress brought it and placed on the table the plate with what appeared — to anyone with our troubled minds — to be piled with steaming dog-doo. We would stare, fixated, at the plate, not daring to look at our comrades, our bodies trembling, shaking, ready to explode. We'd steal a furtive glance at each other, and it would all be over: our shaking table was out of control. And not even the darkest parental threats and imprecations and black looks and head shaking was enough to bring it under control again. The children were dismissed and ordered outside while the adults hurried to finish and depart, before the staff, and fellow diners, realized just how delinquent their angelic children really were, and speculate exactly where they, as parents, had gone wrong.

Our grandparents built their retirement home on the shores of Pleasant Bay on the Cape when I was eight, so from then on, summers were there. Chappy left behind, far away across the Sound. But a magical place like that doesn't really leave you, and I found any new experiences being measured against memories of those island summers.

Christmas cards were our last connection with Lain. Until one summer, almost sixty years after we had left Chappy, my sister and I found ourselves on the Cape at the same time Lain was on Chappaquiddick, and we planned a reunion. Lain took the day ferry from Oak Bluffs to Hyannis, where we met and went on to the Hyannis Yacht Club for lunch.

We sat down at our table, so happy to be catching up. We seemed to have become the same adults our parents had been when we were running wild on Chappy. Was who we were, way back then, in those dreamy summers in the 1950s, gone forever? I had to find out.

"Can anyone finish this jingle," I asked, butting into the flow of the adult conversation. "When things are moving kind of slow . . . . "

In unison we all competed it — "Take Hayley's M.O." — laughing as convulsively as we did back then so that not one of us could speak coherently to tell our poor waitress what we wanted to drink when she came to take our order. Just as we slowly gained our composure, wiping our eyes with our napkins, one of us would ask if Connie Constance had paid a visit with anyone, or if the Baby Dia had come around, keeping us going, as we relived every moment of those long ago magical summers, together, on Chappy.

III
AUNTIE:
THE LAST ROSE OF SUMMER

NEW JERSEY CAN GET HOT IN THE SUMMER. Not just hot. Stifling hot. Filthy hot. Before the days of air conditioning, a big old English Tudor could be as uninhabitable as Guadalcanal. My grandparents for several years had been searching for a summer home somewhere cooler, in New England, and in 1937 happened upon a fifty acre estate on Casco Bay outside of Brunswick, Maine, which they were able to buy at a clearance sale bargain basement Depression era price.

The mansion that once had been there had burned to the ground eight years before; the row of ancient oaks in front still bore scars of that wild nighttime conflagration. The owners had rebuilt in 1930, before the reality of the endless Depression was evident, a handsome Georgian colonial commanding a promontory above the bay, with dramatic views over the islands to Mount Washington in the distance. It had large, formal, high-ceilinged rooms, a sweeping staircase, and came with most of the furnishings. There was a comfortable guest house on the way down to the shore where the owners had stayed as their new house was being built, a barn, chicken coops, a caretaker's cottage out by the road, a large boathouse, and a Chris Craft cruiser moored at the dock, ready to go.

At Ease, as my grandparents called it, became their summer retreat and a playground for their five teenage children. Soon they were improving the property: a formal sunken garden for my grandmother, a racing sloop and an Olympic size salt-water pool down in a field by the bay for the teenagers, stone walls, an apple orchard, cutting gardens, bowling on the green. Over the years it became a special haven for the family, filled with all the memories of a beloved summer place.

To say that the area was rural would give the impression of many more residents than there were. It was, then, when our parents took us to visit our grandparents in the 1950's, an area of forests of tall Bowdin pines and an occasional farmhouse in a clearing. This was the boondocks.

My grandparents' packed dirt drive led off the only road down Harpswell Neck, twisting for three-quarters of a mile through dark woods, until the pines opened up to reveal the beautiful setting above the Bay.

It took helpers to manage a place like that. My grandparents were lucky to find Roy, who did all the maintenance, working there six days a week in season to keep the lawns cut, the bushes trimmed, the gardens photo-shoot ready, the salt-water pool functioning, and the boats ship-shape. Roy's wife, Eva, was the cook, and her dinners were what every guest remembered, even years later. And Esther did the housekeeping. Roy and Eva lived in a century old bungalow on the property, out near the road, and Esther lived with Auntie in a run-down farmhouse just beyond the driveway into *At Ease*. And so it was that one summer when my parents took us to visit our grandmother, by then a widow, Esther invited us to come meet Auntie.

In retrospect, Esther reminded me of young Buddy's cousin in Truman Capote's classic short story, "A Christmas Memory", she was simple like that, kind and wonderful. Esther had been an orphan, nine years old, when adopted by Auntie. They lived together in a farmhouse that looked like it was straight out of Andrew Wyeth's painting "Christina's World". There was no central heating, Esther cut wood for the stove and fireplace; there was no running water, a trusty hand-pump in the sink had been there forever; there was no indoor plumbing, just an outhouse behind the barn. Auntie helped Esther find her way in the world, securing for her a job as a custodian in a nearby school, and with my grandparents when they were there during the summer.

Every morning in the summer, Esther would walk across the field and down the driveway, always in old blue jeans, a faded flannel shirt, a pack of Camels in her top pocket, looking a lot like Willie Nelson — not only her clothes but her weathered face, the two long gray braids knotted at the back of her head, and her eyes, wise old eyes that seemed to see the humor of life. Esther was always accompanied by her dog, Duke, who would wait patiently all day, outside around the house. Esther would come into the house through the garage and up the back stairs to a small servant's room under the eaves, where she would put on a white uniform and begin her duties, making everyone's bed (my first morning there I made the mistake of making mine as I did at home, and Esther took me aside and told me not to do that again, that was her job) and then cleaning and dusting and polishing.

My father had known Esther since he was a teenager, and to him — she always called him "Billy", which delighted me — and to us, she was a fun friend, though in the house — at least in my grandmother's presence — we had to abide by the upstairs/downstairs formalities. But when Esther had a little free time, and my grandmother was away on some errands, we'd urge Esther to join us at the waterfront; we'd all walk down together and wade in the ice cold water of Casco Bay and challenge each other to take a plunge in, which none of us, except my mother, ever worked up the courage to do.

When Esther learned I had just won a prize for a seventh grade science fair project on propagating plants, she invited us to her home to see Auntie's house plants.

As we drove slowly down her rutted driveway that was no more than two weedy, overgrown tracks through a field, Esther came out to greet us and Duke ran over to say hello. She first took us into the barn to show us her goats, which were wandering around, loose. One seemed to be glaring straight at me, getting ready to charge, and, having read all about Billy Goat Gruff in the childhood fairytale, I took no chances and moved behind my father. Esther sensed my fear and tried to coax the goat back into its stall, succeeding only when she tempted it in with a whole pack of her Camels, which the goat munched while staring at me with malevolence.

She then led us into the house, introducing us to Auntie. I'm sure we stayed less than an hour. Yet to this day, I remember Auntie vividly, an elderly lady, tiny, frail-looking, but in no way handicapped, as refined, as gracious, as if she lived in a manor. She showed me her plants — in miscellaneous clay pots on the floor of the sunny hallway into the house — and explained what they were and what they would do, and generously gave me cuttings and clippings and sections from each and told me how to root them. A number of them flourished and grew until, years later, I went off to college.

But it was the main room of their farmhouse that astounded me — dark, with that wonderful smell of old log fires, neat, simple country furniture, with every wall hung with unframed oil paintings on stretched canvases, two, three, four over each other, like in Gertrude Stein's salon in Paris, wonderful landscapes and still lifes, paintings worthy of being shown in the finest galleries.

When she saw us admiring them, Esther, with obvious pride, told us that Auntie had painted them all.

We looked at them in awe. When my mother noted that Auntie had not signed any of the paintings, Auntie chuckled, dismissing this observation with a wave of her hand, telling us she didn't think they were worthy of that. Esther looked at us to see what we thought, and beamed when my parents commented on how fine the paintings were.

I met Auntie only that once. When she was very old and I was very young. I never knew her last name, or, for that matter, her first name — she was always Auntie. Yet in the years — over half a century — since then, I have thought of Auntie often. And wondered. Wondered about many things.

Auntie and Esther didn't have a car; how did they get their food, their provisions? Just walking out their dirt driveway to the road was a hike, and there was nothing along the road for miles in either direction, and then only the smallest of convenience stores. How did they manage? Even if they grew a lot of their food, even if they had milk from their goats and eggs from their chickens, it wouldn't be enough. What was their life like there, in the middle of the twentieth century?

What was Auntie's story? How did this dignified, well-spoken lady — who, Esther later told us, had met Abraham Lincoln's son — how did she find her way to this old farmhouse, to this life, in the middle of nowhere? What was her story?

And of course, I wonder: what if? What if someone long ago had seen her paintings? What if the right someone had seen her work and realized the talent that was there? And been able to lead her in the right direction? To exhibiting her work? To selling her paintings? To refining her style? What might she have achieved? How might her life have been different?

But there her life's work hung, in the least likely of spots, on the walls of a decrepit, weather-beaten farmhouse, in a clearing in the woods, in the middle of nowhere, seen by no one but Esther and an occasional friend or neighbor who stopped in.

I wonder if I might be the last person alive who remembers Auntie?

And I wonder how many more Aunties are out there?

Esther couldn't read or write, but later, when we visited, she pulled out from a cupboard in the kitchen a small notebook, each page with a day of the year. She asked us to write our name on the day that was our birthday, which we each did. "I'll be thinking of you on that day," she told us.

Each year, I sent Esther a card on her birthday and for Christmas, with a little bit of news, knowing that she would have someone read it to her and be proud to show it off to a friend. I did this for years until, after one Christmas, a letter arrived with a return address in Maine and a name I didn't recognize. It was from the person auctioning off the contents of Esther and Auntie's farmhouse, telling me that Esther had died some months before, and reporting on the excitement about the forthcoming auction of authentic country antiques. I wrote and asked if I might purchase one of Auntie's paintings, and the auctioneer was kind enough to send one to me, a lovely landscape of an old wooden bridge over a stream, the colors of the water of the stream, of the sky and clouds, the trees, the fields, so real it could have been a photograph. I had the canvas framed in the gold frame it deserved, which brought out the inner beauty of the painting, and there it hangs, now in my living room, a reminder of Auntie, of Esther, of the old farmhouse, of a summer in Maine long ago. And of the role of fate and luck in what we become, in what becomes of us.

Someone like Auntie always reminds me of the last rose of summer.

No matter what the garden catalogs breathlessly promise about perennials blooming from June to first frost, in real gardens these flowers throw in the towel by September, all except the last brave blossoms of autumn. These are the most beautiful, the ones that appear against all odds, after weeks of frosty mornings and soaking rains that bring down most of the leaves. There, on one of those unexpected dividend days of Indian summer, there, poking through the fallen oak leaves, will be the yellow flower of a Stella d'Oro daylily, one, just one, above the withered stalks and seed pods from the summer's abundance, tiny, smaller than June's but more exquisite in its waxy, orchid-like, solitary perfection, waiting patiently, hopefully, for a sluggish bee making its final rounds in the remaining warmth of high noon. The last Shasta daisy blooming after all the others have given up, the final coreopsis, the last rose, going on, doing its thing against insuperable odds. Aren't they like Mrs. Dubose in Harper Lee's *To Kill a Mockingbird*, the old lady who was determined to break her morphine addiction before she died? That's real courage, Atticus explained to Jem and Scout, "when you know you're licked before you begin but you begin anyway and you see it through no matter what."

These last flowers of autumn, the courageous ones, aren't they the most beautiful of the season? Here, surely, is Tennyson's flower in the crannied wall: "If I could understand / What you are, root and all, and all in all, / I should know what God and man is." To understand these courageous flowers that don't give up, that keep trying even in the most unlikely places and under the most discouraging circumstances, may well be to understand everything.

The flowers of these late bloomers are as remarkable as the stories of life's late bloomers, people like Anna Mary Robertson, better known as Grandma Moses, a hired girl and later the wife of a farmer in New York, who began painting at the age of seventy-six when arthritis made her give up her embroidery. Her canvases were not appreciated as extraordinary works of art until she was into her eighties. Or how about those whose gifts for one reason or another aren't recognized until years and years after they should have been, people like Helen Hooven Santmyer, who, in her thirties, wrote a novel, ". . . *And Ladies of the Club*", which did not find a publisher until half a century later when — at eighty-eight, blind in one eye with a cataract in the other, her eighty-pound body wracked by emphysema and confined to her wheelchair in her book-filled room at Hospitality Home East, a nursing home in her hometown of Xenia, Ohio — she saw her book published to become a best-seller and front-page media event.

But what of someone who, like Eleanor Rigby, was "buried along with her name"? Whose unsigned paintings hung on a wall in a forgotten farmhouse? What then?

Just two words: Emily Dickinson.

How close her strange little poems, written in pencil on scraps of paper, came to oblivion. How close! Terence Davies, the British film maker who wrote "I'm Nobody! Who Are You?" about Emily Dickinson, pondered her lack of recognition in her lifetime: "I just think, oh, why couldn't she have got one success? Or, at least, won first prize for her bread! Why couldn't she have been at the head of the class, for *once*?"

To those who didn't make life's first cut, or second, or third, who weren't genetically endowed to become high school's peppy cheerleaders or homecoming queens or football captains, who weren't accepted at the colleges of their choice, or hired for the jobs they coveted, or granted the acceptance or recognition they deserved, who would never be the awe-inspiring blooms of May and June that elicit all the raves, who went through a lifetime of no one noticing, yet plugged on, who played out with pluck and flair the hand life dealt them, who kept trying, who didn't give up: surely these, the last roses of summer, these are the most beautiful of them all.

IV
WHITECAPS IN WINTER

SOMETIMES, OFF SEASON, I PICTURE MYSELF THERE, at *Whitecaps*, the house my grandparents built over sixty years ago, asleep in the bed in the upstairs room under the eaves, hearing the wind waves pound the side of the house and whistle around the shutters and strum the downpipe by the east corner of the house, while the Bay punches at the base of the bluff below the house, trying to tumble sections into the Bay and consume them, to eventually, inevitably, claim the house as its own.

Throughout the long, dark, endless winter, the house is in hibernation. Life doesn't stop, it still goes on there, but at a quiet pace, almost flat lining, but not quite.

The furnace comes on and turns off throughout the day and night, humming quietly, keeping the house at 50 degrees. The clock with the battery in the living room bookcase, and the ones on the bureaus in the bedrooms, keep time, noting the passage of every minute that passes in each day. Always on Daylight Savings Time, to be ready for the Earth's slow turn on its axis toward Summer. The lights on timers start to come on near the end of the day when what remains of the gloomy light begins to turn dark, first the one in the front hall at 3:30, then the ones in the two back guest rooms, the living room, followed by the dining room, the den, the sunroom, the master bedroom, the room upstairs, the little lamp of Sandwich glass on the small table in the breezeway, some turning off when bedtime comes to each room, others burning bright till morning. The light in the cupula on top of the roof comes on at dusk and shines bright all night, clear nights and nights of fog and wind or frozen nights of snow and sleet, turning off at dawn. Birds alight on the roof as the sun rises. Brave Mr. Fox struts around the yard that is now all his, establishing his familiar paths to check out his domain.

Whitecaps is furnished as summer houses were meant to be, with miscellaneous pieces from parents and grandparents, great grandparents, aunts and uncles, great aunts and uncles from both sides of the family: the marble-topped Victorian table that had been in my great grandmother's apartment, her African violets on it in the sunny narrow hall with lace curtains framing the windows; the carved mahogany bench that had been by the Renaissance Revival library table in my grandparents' English Tudor, where grandchildren sat to crayon their coloring books; an old tavern table that had been in our recreation room, a miscellaneous overlooked piece once piled high with basement clutter that now, polished and waxed, gleams in faded glory by a bedroom window: the dressing table that had been in my grandparents bedroom between the two windows overlooking Casco Bay in Maine; a framed wood carved form of a sailboat in relief that had hung in my father's room when he was a boy.

"I've never seen a house like this," Wendy tells me when she comes with her squad of college student helpers to do a heavy cleaning at the end of the season. She probably has a hundred homes in the area that she takes care of, and all, she reports, have that cookie cutter look — the wicker white furniture covered in navy blue decorated with white anchors, starfish, buoys, lobsters, everything new, everything bare, pristine. "Your house feels like a real home." After more than sixty years there, it does. It is home.

I remember a time we visited my grandfather here, he was living alone still but it wasn't long before he would need helpers, and as we sat around the living room and talked, he waved his hand around the room to encompass everything in it and remarked how we are all renters, that we don't own anything, we are merely renting it for our lifetimes.

I was in high school then, and I sort of understood what he was saying, but not really; I was sure, then, when something was mine, it would be mine for fifty years or more, which, then, seemed as good as forever. Now, of course, I realize how nice it is to think that something we collected, something we used, something we treasured, will be used and cherished by someone else; and how very nice it would be to think that it would remain in the same place where it's always been and be appreciated there for another lifetime. You never know, you can never be sure. But these pieces that have remained where they were for the last sixty years do seem to exude a contentment, a happiness, a permanency, that is almost palpable.

Everything in the waiting house, everything — every piece of furniture, everything hanging on the walls, the photographs, the rugs on the floor, the wallpaper, the paint, the woodwork — carries within it associations, memories, stories.

On the mantle over the fireplace is a ship model of the *Flying Cloud*, the fastest clipper ship that ever sailed the seas, a ship model which was my grandfather's pride and joy. His sister had given it to him when her husband, an avid antique collector, passed away; it had been purchased in the 1920s at auction at Anderson Galleries, a predecessor of Sotheby's. For years, it had been on top of a bookcase in my grandfather's study in New Jersey and I remember whenever our parents took us to visit, my father would lift me up so that I could see it, the sleek lines of the wood, the fine maze of rigging, the tiny anchor and cabin house and lifeboats and ship's wheel, all hand carved, all perfect in every detail, all in exact scale. When my grandparents retired to the Cape, it found its place on the mantle, and my grandfather thought it time to get an appraisal for insurance purposes. He had heard about a well-known ship model maker on the Cape, Robert Innis, and made an appointment to visit him. I tagged along.

I was young then, maybe twelve, and Mr. Innis struck me as elderly, brusque, no-nonsense. As he welcomed us into his house and led us down to his basement workshop, its walls lined with shelves holding his models of clipper ships, barks, frigates, schooners, brigantines, a museum of maritime history, I tried not to stare: he had no right arm.

He told us his story. He was born with one arm, and so had never considered it a handicap. Once, walking the streets of Boston as a young man, he had seen in a store window a primitive ship model with a price tag of $47.50. "Can't be," he said to himself: "I could do better than that." He walked into the store to tell the proprietor that the decimal point on the tag was in the wrong place, that the model, he was sure, was meant to be marked at $4.75.

Assured by the proprietor that it was correctly marked, Mr. Innis said: "I can make as many of these as you want, but even better. Will you buy them from me?"

The proprietor looked at his one arm, shook his head in bemusement, and said words to the effect, "yeah, right."

Innis of course took this as a challenge, went home, and carved his first ship model, tucked it under his arm and brought it back to the store. He put it down on the counter.

"Here it is," he said.

"You're a goddamn liar," the proprietor said, "you didn't make that."

"You want it or not?"

The owner looked it over. "Yes, I think I can sell it."

Innis was prepared to sell it to the shop for $25, but because of the owner's attitude, changed his mind. "A hundred bucks."

"Deal," said the shop owner.

With that, Innis was on his way, carving ever more elaborate models, finding the plans of historical ships in libraries and maritime museums, photocopying them, calculating and reducing the scale, producing ship models snapped up by collectors, auction houses and museums.

My grandfather walked around the basement, shelf to shelf to examine each model, took a few meditative draws on his pipe, made some approving comments and then rendered his verdict.

"Mr. Innis," he said, "these are fine ship models. Very fine indeed. But I have one that's even better."

Innis smirked. "You do, do you? That I have to see."

"I was hoping you'd say that. I want you to come see it and write up an appraisal of it for insurance purposes. Would you do that?"

"Tomorrow morning, 8 a.m."

They shook hands. And the next morning, 8 a.m. sharp, Mr. Innis had parked in the driveway and was knocking on our door.

My grandfather showed him in.

"Where is it?" Innis demanded, and without further ado was led into the living room to the mantle.

He stood back, looked at it, then approached it, his eyes within inches of the *Flying Cloud*, scanning it from bow to stern.

"Where did you get this?"

My grandfather explained it's provenance.

Innis grinned. "It's one of mine. I made this ship model. Look at this."

He then proceeded to show us his signature marks.

"Well I'll be damned," my grandfather muttered. "I'll be damned."

Will the next person who owns the *Flying Cloud* maybe sense some of this back story, some of this history? Will their own history enrich it even more?

Off season, when I dream of *Whitecaps*, my dreams are often of being there in the summer. It is a late afternoon. I'm sitting on a deck chair under the pines, looking out over the bluff thick with salt spray rose, fragrant with those white flowers and plum flowers, down the bay to the islands, and beyond, all along the horizon, the white dunes of the outer beach, and through hollows between the dunes, the deep blue of the sea. Terms are hovering over the shallows, diving for tinker mackerel, and gulls are flying back and forth to the islands, and fair weather clouds drift out over the bay, with shadows of clouds floating on the water. There is always a breeze through the pines on top of the bluff where I sit, and I can hear the breakers booming up and down the empty miles of outer beach, a steady muffled faraway hypnotic roar.

But now, off season, winter is in the roar, and the house waits patiently for another summer.

V
ROUGHHOUSING

Remember those summer storms?

We always knew they were brewing if the wind was blowing up the leaves of the poplars along the shore when we took our morning walks. Just like this morning.

Remember how all day it would feel like a storm was coming in? And the small craft warning flag would be flying at the lighthouse? As it is today.

The sky and Bay are timber wolf gray. Packs of waves with livid whitecap fangs race and leap down the channel, snapping and biting at Stinkin Hummock and trying to tear loose from its mooring our frightened catboat. These waves mean business. We've been caught out in them before and know they want to kill. As I look up from my book, out the picture window in the sunroom, I think of the director of the sailing camp down the Bay, who had sailed these waters for forty years; he was out on his *Sailfish* when waves like these picked up. It was several days before his body was found on the backside of one of the islands. No, better be snug inside when a nor'easter howls in from the sea.

On the wall of the sunroom, the wind indicator light glowers orange, flashing north, northeast, north, northeast, east, northeast.

Now rain lunges at the picture window, pounces on the roof, growls through the gutters.

"Someone take Amy out," my mother calls from the kitchen, "she hasn't been out since this morning."

My father is in the den with the game on. I look over at Marjorie, curled up asleep on the loveseat. Golden Retriever Amy is

45

luxuriously stretched out on the carpet, dozing and listening to the storm.

It's my turn, I know, but it's worth a try anyhow.

"Your mother wants someone to take the dog out," I say to Marjorie.

"It's your turn," she mumbles from somewhere far away, her eyes closed shut.

It is, so I don't press the issue.

"OK, Amy, it's us," I say, reluctantly laying down *The Widow's Walk* and getting out of that particularly comfortable old Victorian rocker, the one that had been in my great grandmother's apartment, the upholstered one with the big springs under the wooden rockers. Just thinking of going out in the storm I can feel the claws of rain scratching at the back of my neck.

"We're going to brave this gale and go out there and do our business, right Amy?"

Amy doesn't budge. Having learned from the master, she closes her eyes, just like Marjorie, and feigns deep sleep.

"OK, Amy, here we go!" I say, trying to make it sound like an adventure.

For a water dog who will splash into the Bay any time, any season, Amy abhors a sprinkle of rain on her head. To even think of going out in a nor'easter clearly is out of the question. She's nestled in for the duration.

"What? Are you like some big old house cat, afraid to get wet?" I ask in utter amazement. "A big old Maine coon pussy cat?"

A cheap trick, but that catches her attention. Without too much enthusiasm, she raises up just enough to look toward the picture window to see if there really is — and she does have serious doubts about this — a cat dumb enough to be outside in the pouring rain.

Let's get this done, whatever it takes, I think to myself, anxious to go out, come in, dry off and get back to my murder mystery. Maybe it's time for an old-fashioned cat scare.

I rush up to the window and look out at the storm.

"It *is* a *cat*!" I call to Amy with concern. "A *big cat*!"

From drowsy slumber to red alert in an instant, she's up and at the window, looking. *Where? Where?*

Cat scares are getting a little old, but just often enough there actually is a suspicious-looking cat out there, lurking across the lawn, stalking the quail. So it is essential for us to check out each alarm. We race from the sunroom through the living room, picking up speed as we pass through the kitchen with Amy's toenails skating over the floor. In the breezeway I grab an umbrella, and we're out on the patio, Amy at attention, looking here and there in the deluge for a sight of the evil, soggy feline intruder.

"There, I saw it there!" I say, pointing out to the bluff with my umbrella held against the wind blowing the rain straight in at the house.

The sounds of wind whipping through the pines on the bluff and waves tearing down the channel and rain lashing against the house mix in a menacing howl.

"Hurry," I urge Amy, "hurry!"

Amy senses she might have been tricked but, as not to lose face, trots out to the top of the bluff, gives a perfunctory look around for trouble, and then, finding none and knowing I'm watching intently, at least goes through a pantomime of doing what she's supposed to do (a pantomime I'm convinced on occasion she performs to get those who are obsessively concerned with her bodily functions off her back). Then, her ears blowing about like windsocks, lickety-split, she tears back to the shelter of the house.

I lock the door behind us against the storm.

In the breezeway she gives a good, deliberate head to tail shake, spraying off the rain. And that is that. She heads back to the sunroom, dark now but for the light from the table lamp by my rocker, and resumes her nap that was so rudely interrupted.

"Did you dry her with a towel?" my mother calls from the kitchen a few minutes after I'm settled in the rocker and am back into my Nantucket murder mystery.

"What?"

"Did you dry the dog with a towel?"

"Damn," I mutter.

"Make sure her chest is dry," my mother reminds me as I walk out to the back hall to get from the bottom of the closet the old orange bath towel. "The chest is the most important part to get bone dry."

Now, since the time when man first invited dog to come live in his house, there has always been a lot of give and take in making this cross-species relationship work. At times, the relationship can be so close that we believe dogs are very much like us, that we, indeed, are related, that we're parents or children, brothers or sisters. And dogs, studies have shown, watch us and know us better than we know them. Maybe dogs find that we become more like them, and maybe we do. They adopt us into their packs as we adopt them into our families. Yet there will always be things about dogs we just cannot comprehend, like what it is that so ecstatically delightful in sliding into something dead and smelly and squishing it up real tight behind the ears, just as there must be many things about us that dogs cannot fathom, like the endless wasted hours we spend seated before the flickering images in a big black box.

With few exceptions, what Amy might not fully understand, she gamely accepts. And one of those few exceptions is getting toweled dried. For the supreme leader of a pack to be dried off behind the ears and have her tummy rubbed dry after being outside in the rain is, to her, completely incomprehensible and unreasonable. Clearly it is unacceptable.

Carrying the orange bath towel into the sunroom is like pirou-etting with a red cape through the streets of Pamplona during the running of the bulls. As soon as Amy sees it coming, she charges it, grabbing hold of a corner, and, hanging on, shakes it like a partridge. She has her end, I have mine, with which I quickly go to work.

"Oh, nice and dry, we're going to get you so nice and dry," I sing-song chant, toweling under each ear and around her throat. "Ohh-hhh, so beautiful, such beautiful, lovely, luscious golden hair, so soft and silky, golden blond, honey blond, lustrous honey blond hair, uummmm, so smooth and soft."

Nodding slowly in agreement, she momentarily succumbs to this soothing beauty shop lullaby, almost letting her end of the towel drop from her mouth.

She catches herself just as it does, and grabs it with a snap.

"Amy get dry," I patiently explain, prying open her jaws and pulling out the gooey end, only to have her lunge for another hunk of it.

She looks up at me to see how I'm taking it.

"Now wait a minute," I indignantly protest. "Wait just a min-ute! They wouldn't put up with this in a beauty parlor, and you know it."

With her hanging onto one end of the towel, all the while slyly waiting to reel in more if I relax my hold on it, I work with the few square inches of towel she's left me, drying around the ears, under the chin, down the chest, the back, the tail, the legs, rolling her over on her back to get the stomach. Swishing her tail back and forth, her black lips grinning, she grabs more towel, which she holds in her jaws and flails with her paws.

"This is so silly, Amy. Why would a dog even think of something like this? What would a dog? What would a dog even be thinking?" I ask Amy in astonishment as she rolls back over on her stomach, tugging at her end of the towel and staring right at me, defiantly.

"What's she doing?" Marjorie asks, wide awake now that all the dirty work has been done and the fun might be beginning.

"I think she's being defiant. To me, at least," I say, tugging at my end of the towel to get more back, "this smacks of defiance. Do we have to take it?"

"No we do not," Marjorie states empathically, descending from the loveseat to the carpet to the scene of impending battle. "Give me that end."

Let the games begin.

"Is she dry?" my mother calls in, not fully appreciating the enormity of the task she has assigned. To her, Amy always is a little girl who can be dressed up in ribbons and ruffles for tea parties, a sweet little girl all sugar and spice and everything nice.

"Yup. As dry as she's going to get," I answer.

"Did you get the chest? The chest is the most important."

"It's as dry as I can get it."

I neglect to report that our beauty parlor patron is currently engaged in a rousing game of tug-of-war, with Marjorie now manning the other end of the orange towel.

Already the game is getting pretty intense.

"Amy, you're a brute and you know it," Marjorie says.

All golden retrievers like to fantasize that they can be fierce, and Amy redoubles her tugging.

"Come'on, one hand," I tell my sister. "Give her a chance."

"Give her a chance? Give her a chance?" she hisses at me, hanging onto the towel for dear life. "This is not a retriever you brought back in. This is some kind of wolf dog. That's loose in the house."

And sure enough, Amy's lovely and loving brown eyes have assumed the frightening steely glint of the Big Bad Wolf's eyes in that split second when Little Red Riding Hood suddenly perceived that it was not Grandmama under the covers.

"One hand, one hand, those are the rules," I remind her again. "She's only got one mouth."

"OK, OK," my sister mutters, letting go with one hand and instantly losing several inches of towel as Amy pulls back against the momentary slack.

"I told you! She's not playing fair."

"She's playing fair, and she's going to beat you if you don't watch out."

Now the match gets serious, and a gambling man in that dark room with the wind wailing about the eaves would have had a hard time knowing where to place his bet: on a Wellesley graduate sprawled on the floor, one end of a towel clenched in her hand, pulling for all she was worth, or on a wiley retriever with the other end of the towel clenched in barred teeth, her eyes becoming more and more demonic, a low warning rumbling from her throat, watching, watching, waiting for that split second of weakness, a moment of exhaustion, a repositioning,

Now!

In a movement almost too quick to see, Amy lets go of the towel and pounces on it several inches closer to the middle, an ominous growl in her throat defying anyone to call that cheating; and is that a look of triumph in her eye?

"See! I told you! That's cheating!" my sister declares.

Bully on you, Amy seems to reply as she repeats her tactic and lunges again at the towel, grabbing it inches from my sister's fingers.

Marjorie lets go as if she's touched a mouse crouched in the dusty dark corner of a cupboard, and jumps back.

"Good gods, Amy, you win. OK? I quit. You win. You can have the stupid towel. It's yours."

Amy already knows she has won without waiting for that gracious concession speech. She grabs my sister's end of the towel, lying over the rest of it, and begins a methodical ripping, viciously shaking a hunk.

Game over, right? Amy has won fair and square, everyone is ready to concede that. But woe be unto whoever tries to retrieve that towel. This is the really hard part of the game.

Left to her devices, Amy will make a great show of angrily ripping loose every thread of the hated towel, mash around a bunch until they're nice and soggy, and then swallow, which isn't good for the drying towel or for a golden retriever. Our mission impossible is to take the towel away and let it dry out for another rainy day.

"Here, get the towel," I breezily tell my sister as if it's the simplest matter in the world.

"Are you crazy? I'm not going near it," she says from the safety of the loveseat, her bare feet tucked under her. "You get it."

Amy is waiting for just such an eventuality, her eyes challenging anyone who comes within five feet of her. Any closer and she lets go of the towel and assumes her protective position, huddling over it, closer still and a warning snarl, then a wrinkling of the nose, a show of fierce retriever teeth, the hair on the back of her neck magically rises, and if anyone is foolish enough to lay even a finger on a stray corner of that towel: Attack! The most ferocious, fiercest, most blood curdling snarl and lunge at those misplaced fingers as if she meant to tear them out at the roots.

Amy never actually connects with human flesh, perhaps because she doesn't really intend to and is merely training us to be fair. Or perhaps she is just having some fun bullying us (she always seems to chuckle to herself as soon as she snarls and, like the gracious winner of a heated tennis match, trots right over to shake hands). Or maybe under these circumstances of imminent peril, misplaced human fingers can retreat pretty quickly. But her response always is the same. And, upon reflection, it does make sense: she has won the game, fair and square. The trophy is hers. That is retriever fairness. And who could argue with that?

But there is still the matter of getting the towel back while it still resembles a towel and not merely its constituent threads. As Mr. Darling in *Peter Pan* learned with Nana, all the sweet talk in the world will get you nowhere. Fair, after all, is fair. To the victor belongs the spoils.

It's time to play our trump card: cheese.

Like old Ben Gunn marooned on Treasure Island, Amy dreams of cheese, long sweet, deliciously repetitive dreams of cheese. For a good morsel of cheese, there isn't anything she won't do.

We know it will work.

"Would you like a piece of cheese?" we ask as she glares at us, awaiting our next move,

She looks at us, suspiciously, considering our offer, still holding the towel firmly in clenched jaws, not about to be fooled by the old Trojan Horse ploy.

"No, really. A little bit of *cheese*?"

It always helps to describe exactly what kind of cheese we're talking about.

"We've got some of that new sharp Cheddar *cheese*. Yup, the strong kind. From Vermont. It's pretty good *cheese*."

The towel is dropped, long forgotten, the last thing on her mind. Who wants a dry, tasteless towel when there's cheese being distributed?

She's up. She's herding us toward the kitchen six inches from our legs, faster, faster. Must get that *cheese*.

Into the bright kitchen she skips, as sweet and innocent as little Miss Muffet, her wolf mask put away. Straight to the refrigerator where fabulous stashes of cheese are stored. Out comes the slab of golden cheese from the back of the refrigerator door. It is laid on the counter. Two brown eyes watch in salivating anticipation, like Ben Gunn's, as it is placed on a bread board, the wrapper opened, a paring knife taken from a drawer, a nice hunk neatly cut from it and, like a pirate's gold bar, divided into thirds.

"What's that for?" my mother asks.

"We had to promise her cheese to get the towel back," my sister explains.

"Oh, don't be ridiculous," my mother responds. "She always lets me dry her, don't you Amy? Amy, you have them buffaloed, that's what I think."

A tasty morsel of strong Vermont Cheddar cheese, down the hatch in a gulp. And a healthy half of the other two pieces from the tug-of-war losers.

Pots bubble and simmer on the stove.

The smell of chicken roasting in the oven catches Amy's interest. She looks up at my mother, expectantly, as if to ask, "*Is there anything I can do to help in the kitchen? Is it ready yet? Can I have a piece now?*" Amy knows by heart the answers to each of these kitchen questions, but her philosophy is that it never hurts to ask again. And she knows, too, that at dinnertime, merely by resting her head in our laps and poking her nose into the stomachs of those pack members she can so easily dominate, she will secure all the chicken she wants, no hunting or skinning required.

Our work is done. We're in for the night, cozy and warm.

The orange towel is out of sight, having been secreted in the washing machine.

Everyone is content.

We three head back to the sunroom to resume our dozing and sleeping and reading, as outside the wind drives sheets of rain against the house, as if the storm will blow all night, and through the next day.

VI
SNOW DAY

IT DOESN'T SEEM TO SNOW ANYMORE the way it once did. Of course, when I was growing up, weather forecasting had none of the computer-model sophistication it has today; a hurricane would slam into a coastal town that wasn't ready for it, and snow would arrive without warning. As a result, children back then seemed to have much more of an influence over the direction and intensity of a storm, so that an elementary school filled with students intent on a snow day could — just as a lightning rod attracts lightning — actually draw a blizzard into town.

Maybe we had some sixth sense about storms. Maybe, like animals, we could feel a change in atmospheric pressure and sense when a storm was approaching. However, we did it, we always seemed to know with uncanny prescience when a big one was on the way. We knew just what sort of day was a blizzard breeder, the necessary weight and texture of the clouds, the exact sickly gray-yellow hue of the sky, the specific temperature that would be best, the precise feel of the air. And when these conditions converged, our teacher would be hard-pressed to keep our attention as we'd sneak glances out the oak-framed windows to make sure the conditions held, passing folded notes to establish the telephone chain if someone learned that school was closing.

To get the kind of accumulation we needed, the snow would have to start in earnest by suppertime, and it had to be the right kind of snow. Several times between supper and bed — repeatedly, actually — my sister and I would turn off all the lights in a room and pull back the curtain to check how it was doing. None of that Robert Frost "easy wind and downy flake" stuff for us; nor were big wet flakes acceptable, or snow that fell tentatively, like it was finishing up for the night. Such snow would be shamed by our hisses and boos. We were looking for a snow with a seriousness of purpose, a heavy, hard, steady snow that wasn't going anyplace anytime soon, and we'd fall into sweet sleep with its steady swish against the storm windows.

Instantly, on waking, we'd know even before we looked. There wouldn't be a sound. Not a car passing by. Not the push and scrape of a snow shovel. Not the grinding rumble of the city's snowplows. Total, absolute, pristine, wonderful silence, which could mean only that the snow was so deep it had shut down the city. Snow Day!

Snow stuck to the storm windows, covering them. This was a good sign; there must be just enough moisture in it for perfect snowmen, for snowballs and forts. A dash to a window in the front of the house: outside, a silent snowbound Currier & Ives winter morning. We were expert surveyors then, and by bouncing from window to window, we took all the necessary sitings and triangulations to gauge its depth — eighteen inches, a good two feet at least, two and a half, three feet, as high as the top step out the front door, higher than the wall around the terrace at the back of the house, deep enough to turn the bushes by the porch into mounds, and, down the side of the driveway, wind-swirled drifts that could cover a car. Oh, yes, this was a Snow Day, no questions asked, no debate about it, no worrying that there would be a disappointing delayed opening. This was a Snow Day, and maybe even, with a little luck, a two-day cleanup.

As Mole in *The Wind in the Willows* knew, "the best part of a holiday is perhaps not so much to be resting yourself, as to see all the other fellows busy working." A Snow Day was even better than that; it was an unexpected holiday for everyone, a gift of a pure day. Whatever had been planned had to be canceled, no explanations or apologies required. What errands and chores should have been done, couldn't be. We were isolated by the storm, enveloped togeth-er in the house, with a fire in the fireplace and a long do-nothing day stretching endlessly ahead: a Snow Day was more wonderful than a Saturday or Sunday, or any holiday.

After breakfast, shoveling out was the first order of business. By the time our mother made sure we were properly outfitted in bulky layers of heavy woolen clothes, shirts and sweaters and stiff warm coats, snow pants with straps that went under the foot, those black galoshes that buckled up the front, cumbersome mittens and itchy ski caps covered over with a hood tied too tight under the chin — attire that would have been excessive for explorers on a three-month expedition across the ice floes of the Arctic — we would have agreed to do anything to get outside. The idea of shoveling seemed an ad-venture, humanity against the elements, and off we waddled down the stairs to the garage to get the shovels.

Opening the garage door was like raising the curtain on a spec-tacular stage setting: the storm had taken away our familiar world and replaced it with the Yukon. Either we were a lot shorter then, or those snows truly were monumental, for it was all we could do to hopscotch through the virgin depths up the drive to where the sidewalk should be, and, shovelful by shovelful, begin to clear a sin-gle-width path through the snow into the house.

There were always gangs of older boys (dressed only in flannel shirts and jeans, with a ski band around their ears, boots flapping open) who'd come house-to-house to shovel driveways for a few dol-lars and neaten up our wavering paths where we thought the side-walk, more or less, should be; so there was plenty of time to get on to the real business of building the forts from which bombardments would be launched and repulsed. If the conditions were just right, you could cut out building blocks from the snow in the backyard and stack them up and smooth them together, igloo-fashion, to con-struct a pretty formidable fort that would be stocked with rounds of snowballs. Later, when a truce was called, the old wooden toboggan our parents had when they were growing up was hauled out of the furnace room for rides down the hill along the side of the house, all the way to the back of the yard, and once that path was established, the runway was perfect for the sleds and plastic flyers.

By dusk, when our neighbors started drifting home and we had filled the bird feeders with sunflower seed and suet, the buckles of our galoshes were embedded with snow and ice, ice pellets stuck to our mittens and filled our shoes and socks, and every layer of clothing was pretty well soaked with sweat and snow and smelled like wet wool.

We'd sit by the fireplace with mugs of hot chocolate laced with marshmallows, as the oak-log embers sputtered and flared colors when our father tossed in a handful of the special salt powder. And we would gaze and try to read in the flicker of the flames whether school would be closed again tomorrow.

VII
CURING SNOW MADNESS

WHEN WE WERE YOUNG, January snow froze solid and stayed around, day after day, getting older, more scarred, pitted, stained, finally overstaying its welcome until it became as tiresome and oppressive, as maddening, as the snows of Willa Cather and O. E. Rolvaag.

Physicians didn't talk about it, but it was a fairly simple matter to self-diagnose when you were coming down with snow madness. The symptoms were obvious and easy to spot. Complexions assumed the waxy tallow sheen of candles. You felt too hot inside the house and too cold outside. Family members began casting black looks at you as if, when arguing about the most inconsequential trivialities — which was all that was talked about then — they were contemplating an intervention, an exorcism, or at least setting your mattress ablaze as you slept. You began to feel an uncomfortable physical pressure in being housebound, and when you stepped outside to escape the pressure, you felt hemmed in by frozen drifts that loomed above the narrow walkways. Every single time you passed the Burton house, you stared at the discolored spot in the snow where a dog had relieved itself weeks ago, and by the corner of the Picketts' driveway, you kicked at that annoying jagged edge of ice, trying again to break it off, and again hurt your toes, and again stomped at it with your heel, and still the accursed chunk wouldn't break off, and the sound of the snow crunching under your feet became as grating as Mr. Stoltz dragging his fingernails across the science classroom blackboard, and you tracked in grit and salt. Life had become mere existence. Bundled up, winter-weary, you plodded along day after day. "Spring is too far away to comfort even by anticipation," Joseph Wood Krutch wrote of these depressing days, "and winter long ago lost the charm of novelty. This is the very three A.M. of the calendar."

When such symptoms persisted for more than a week or two and you felt yourself teetering close to the abyss of snow madness, a sure antidote was to visit one of the local greenhouses. My favorite was a rather small one attached to a garden center and gift shop where, the snowy January I was in the seventh grade, I went to buy plants and supplies for my science-fair project.

To open that door from the gift shop into the greenhouse was to walk right into a tropical rain forest, a humid, fragrant jungle so impenetrable that a pith helmet and machete seemed appropriate. Lush, shiny leaves and feathery fronds spilled over every wooden table, poked out from under the benches, crept over the mossy white pebbles of the walkways, pushed up and out at the glass. There were bushes whose branches were laden with miniature oranges, tables of African violets with white, pink, and purple flowers, benches of strangely shaped, succulent cacti protected by fearsome spikes that made you tingle just looking at them, trays of tiny seedlings and coleus cuttings, palms growing up from giant pods, the sensuous waxy flowers of hibiscus and vining jasmine, ferns hanging from the ceiling, tumbling in luxuriant profusion, coffee plants and ginger plants and snake plants and philodendron with smooth leaves and variegated leaves and jagged indented leaves, geraniums, a Christmas cactus cascading with orchidlike flowers, an enormous rubber tree that must have been decades old, plants with curious fleshy leaves and fuzzy leaves and knobby spiked leaves that had to be touched, a trellis here and there tangled in vines of exotic unknowns. And the heavy moist air held the wonderful fragrance of damp sphagnum moss and potting soil and sand, the citrus of the lemon trees, April's aroma of hyacinth, the green chlorophyll smell of leaves, of growing, of living, of life.

Scurrying in and out of this jungle was a wiry old man who, at his workbench in the corner of the greenhouse covered with a jumble of projects, seemed to me as remarkable as a medieval alchemist. I remember Ted always in a red plaid flannel shirt, a ubiquitous pack of *Camels* in his shirt pocket. He had, always, a day-old white stubble, dirt packed under his fingernails, and his hands, constantly moving, looked as though they would always be the color of potting soil, even if scrubbed and scrubbed.

Ted was absorbed in his work and would let customers wander around his greenhouse for as long as they wanted without bothering them. But when he learned I was working on a science project about the propagation of plants, those preoccupied eyes behind the thick glasses with heavy black frames became the eyes of a fellow seventh grader opening up a much-hoped-for chemistry set on Christmas morning.

I had been working that winter on our jalousied side porch, planting seeds saved from the Halloween pumpkin and breakfast grapefruit and oranges, poking toothpicks into an avocado and suspending it in a glass of water, collecting spores from the underside of fern fronds and germinating them in a terrarium, cutting off the tops of carrots and turnips and a slice of a potato and watching them grow into new plants. Ted took me on a crash graduate-level course in botany. He showed me how to unpot a snake plant and divide it into five plants, how to take a leaf from a rex begonia, cut some slits into the veins of the leaf, fasten it down on the soil with unbent paper clips, and wait for roots and leaves to form. He explained what vermiculite and perlite were, and in what proportions they should be mixed with potting soil or soil from the garden; the differences between clay pots and plastic pots; how rooting hormones were best applied in making cuttings; the uses of fertilizers and plant foods. He knew the Latin names of all the plants in his greenhouse and used them conversationally until they became as familiar as my own.

He taught me how to take a gratula plant and cut off a ring of bark on one branch, rub the cut with Rootone, wrap the cut in sphagnum moss and surround the moss with plastic held on by rubber bands. A new plant would grow at the incision. I watched, as I would have watched Dr. DeBakey perform open-heart surgery, as Ted grafted a section of an oxilo tree cactus (the scion) onto an obruntal cactus (the stock).

That winter our side porch became a plant laboratory, the wooden shelf along the windows covered pot to pot with experiments. I dug through the snow and hacked out a bedraggled pachysandra, brought it into the garage for a day to thaw, cut the roots into pieces, and planted them to see if they would grow. Epsicia runners were held down in another pot to root. Geranium cuttings were placed side by side in water, potting soil and vermiculite to see which grew the best. Endless variations of sun and shade were tested, varying amounts of rooting hormone were applied, measurements of roots and shoots were taken with the precision of an ophthalmologist, experiments were conducted in hydroponics and in growing plants under artificial light.

The creation of this home greenhouse, and the frequent visits to Ted's that the science project necessitated, no doubt staved off any serious seizures of snow madness that long, cold winter.

No longer can you get into your car on a winter's day and be in an Ecuadorian rain forest in ten minutes. Ted's greenhouse and the whole garden center of which it was a part are long gone; a concrete and glass office building and huge parking lot now occupy that sunny spot. The Veteran's greenhouse on Mountain Avenue, where we'd buy fresh-cut carnations, was demolished years ago for more suburban homes. And Mary McDonald's greenhouses across from the school are gone now, too. Now flowers and plants are shipped in overnight from places where they're less expensive to grow, and it's almost easier to fly to Ecuador than to find a greenhouse nearby.

Today doctors diagnose the melancholy-inducing days of January as seasonal affective disorder and note its symptoms as depression, a craving for carbohydrates, excessive sleeping and social withdrawal, and treat it with light therapy, exposing the patient to strong light to try to trick the brain into thinking it's not really winter. Maybe that works, though walking into the dry cleaners on a January day of freezing drizzle and sleet, smelling spring and seeing the narcissus in bloom on the counter, can sometimes provide all the fix you need.

VIII
PLANT PORN

PURVEYORS OF PLANT PORNOGRAPHY are more sinister, more so-
phisticated, more insidious than the raunchiest merchants of old
Forty-Second Street. They print their lurid catalogs months in ad-
vance and address them to those whose names have been culled
from mailing lists of individuals known to be pitifully weak and sus-
ceptible to temptation. Then, like loathsome predators, they lie in
wait, monitoring the long-range weather forecasts for the right day
to flash their wares.

We know from experience exactly what day it will be, though
because of our proclivities, we never are able to marshal our defens-
es to "just say no." It will be, invariably, inevitably, a winter's day, not
any winter's day but specifically Robert Frost's "darkest evening of
the year" day, a dreary day of overcast gloom and cold gray drizzle.
By late afternoon it's already so dark it could be night. And that's
when you hear it.

You look up from your desk, startled. And listen. No, it can't be:
that insistent tinkling on your cold windowpane sounds like sleet.

You turn out the lights in your office and close the door so you
can see outside. It's not a pretty sight. In the pale penumbra of the
parking lot's cold fluorescent lights, fellow workers are leaving the
building, cautiously walking over shiny blacktop. Already the grass
around the parking lot is whitening. A woman bundled like a Russian peasant in quilted coat and winter boots teeters, almost slips,
rights herself, and then proceeds as if on a balance beam, baby step
by baby step, out to her car. Others are turning on their engines,
opening their trunks, digging out their scrapers and working on the

windshields glazed with ice, their coats buttoned up around their necks, their scarves and hair blowing about, the exhaust from tailpipes whipped into the dark.

Scrape, scrape, scrape: you hear that rasping, spine-tingling sound even here, on the third floor, the sound of ice thick enough to skate on being chipped and cracked from glass. The first cars slip and skid as they come to the stop sign at the bottom of the hill. In the distance, sirens sound. The police and rescue squads will be working overtime tonight.

The commuter's dilemma: leave now, before it gets any worse? Or wait until the rush-hour traffic clears? Like a dutiful Bob Cratchit, you go back to work, but before long, you look outside again. Now it's not just the grass beyond the lot that's white. The ice on the parking lot has been covered over with snow, it's coming down now, and workers are pouring out of the building as if it grazed an iceberg, took on a nasty list, and is about to capsize. Raised eyebrows and scowls of oh-so-dedicated and foolhardy fellow workers notwithstanding, it's every man for himself, the women and children be damned: abandon ship!

Outside, it's even worse than it looked. Your feet feel the ice under the snow, and as you turn the heater on high and leave the dark cocoon of the car to brush off snow and scrape ice as quickly as possible before more accumulates, your devise your game plan. The sanders and plows haven't come by yet; are the roads even passable? You have good tires, a heavy car, a full tank, front-wheel drive. Slow, steady, keep the forward momentum going, and you'll get home when you get home.

It's working. You feel the treachery of the roads but compensate by crawling along in low gear, following in the tracks of the car ahead, not too close so you won't have to stop suddenly, just steady, inch by inch, homeward bound, humming a rendition of Scarlett O'Hara's refrain: "Just a few more miles to tote the weary load." The other commuters must be of like mind, for a slow, orderly procession of cars winds its way along the road through the storm.

And then! Out of the swirling snowy mists, appears from nowhere a car ahead of you, you know which one, the same one that, like the abominable snowman, makes its mysterious appearance in every blizzard as commuters struggle home. Yes, it's that one, the big old boat of a car ahead of you, the one you just know won't be able to surmount the slight rise in the road no steeper than a stack of five or six paper napkins.

"You can do it, old man," you find yourself saying aloud, though is its driver a man? Maybe. Could it be a woman? Perhaps. All you can see through the thud of your frozen wipers, fighting to keep open a diminishing amount of windshield, is a huge head and some sort of furry coat, which, come to think of it, is the exact description mountaineers have provided of their glimpses of the abominable snowman in the high reaches of the Himalayas.

"Steady, old man, just take it nice and steady, don't stop, as long as you don't stop, you'll be okay, just keep — "

The red brake lights flash on, the car goes into a sickening, erratic skid, stops, and then ("No! No! Please don't do it") the driver guns his engine.

Wheels spin and dig into snow and ice. What to do next? (No! No! I beg of you, please don't!") Why, step on the gas again, this time harder, longer. The wheels are smoking, the car shudders, trembles, then settles deeper into the ice grave it's digging. What now? Now you only shake your head in silent benediction. You know it's all over as Yeti goes for the big one: floor it! A horrible, storm-rending screech as the car pours on more thrust than would be necessary to get a 747 airborne off an aircraft carrier. But a car is not a 747, and now the worst sound of all: silence. The car's lights flicker out. Did he blow his engine? Has he given up? Did the carbon monoxide from his attempted interplanetary launch do him in? Is he going to sit there and wait out the storm? You look in the rearview mirror: the glow of a line of cars extending as far down the road as you can see. Of course, someone honks his horn. Yes, that will help. Then, farther down the line, another horn answers, either telling the first horn to knock it off or seconding the motion. Soon, way down the line, others join in; not all together but one then another and another, until a grating, maddening rhythm develops.

There is nothing to be done. Yeti has quite completely blocked the road, his car having come to its final resting place in a peculiarly perpendicular position. The line of cars traveling the opposite direction, in orderly fashion, slowing to do a bit of rubbernecking, make pulling out and around impossible. Yeti is stuck. You are stuck. They are stuck. We are all stuck.

Snow is falling faster. Your wipers fight the good fight, but on each downward sweep, they compress the heavy snow into solid-pack ice that, minute by minute, grows higher up the windshield, cutting visibility. The side windows are covered, and the back window, despite the window heater, offers only a hazy glimpse of the spectral white lights behind you. It's dark inside the car. Against the hiss of snow and sleet and the breathing of the heater, the horns begin to sound far away, soothing, almost like a lullaby. You settle back in the seat. "The woods are lovely, dark, and deep," your mind hums, "the woods are lovely dark and — ". You sit up with a start: carbon-monoxide poisoning? You open the window to let in some fresh air, and soon the two fingers on your left hand that were frostbitten years ago begin to feel rubbery. Can't sit here forever. Got to get out of here. Now! Got to get out! Losing it! The edges of panic have set in, and around those edges new plans begin to take shape. Abandon car on side of road and walk home. Ten miles in a blizzard can be a long way; remember Per Hansa. Gun the engine and ram Yeti off the road. Your car could get damaged, and you don't have time next week to take it to the shop. Very slowly move forward and shove him sideways out of —

Wait! Yeti has climbed out. He is looking around. He huddles back in. His lights flicker on, he guns the engine. Again. And again. The car rocks and rolls and, with a roar and a lurch, breaks free from its ice coffin and moves forward into the snow.

Thank you, thank you, you pray, putting your car in drive, erasing forward, feeling the wheels spin on the ice and then catch, rumbling and crunching over the mysterious yeti tracks and then onward. You reinstate your game plan, reviewing it to follow a maze of back roads and side streets, risking drifts of virgin snow to avoid any more encounters with abominable snowmen.

At last you reach your driveway, though the journey is not over, Tara still lies ahead. The driveway goes pretty much straight up, angling along the side of the ridge, and one slip of the wheels over the snow-covered Belgian-block edge and the car will roll down the embankment, flip over on the road, slide down the ridge, landing on its roof far below in the woods, bursting into flames, as in the best action flick. So no power will drain from the engine, you shut down the wipers, the heater, the defroster the back-window heater, take a running start, and plow up that drive through the ice and snow, the car quivering halfway up, the wheels veering the wrong way, toward the Belgian-block edge, don't stop, don't stop, can't stop or it's all over, straighten, straighten, the wheels spin, on, on, one hand off the wheel, don't stop, press the garage-door opener, the garage-door swings up, keep going, the beckoning light in the garage urges you on, on car, toward that lovely, warm, welcoming orifice, into it, front wheels grasp the dry floor of the garage, you're in, home, you got it, you turn off the engine, unfasten your hands finger by finger from the wheel, and inhale, realizing at last that you've been holding your breath for quite some time. Feeling not unlike Sir Ernest Shackleton after his voyage in an open boat across Antarctica, you stumble out of the car, close the garage door, and go into the house.

It's that kind of night. So when you open the front door and take in the mail, the fact that this is the night the plant predators have earmarked to tempt you is the last thing on your mind. You are thankful to be home out of the storm, thankful that the power hasn't been knocked out by the ice, thankful that heat is coming up, thankful that the oven is warming and that there are enough leftovers for an easy dinner, thankful that tomorrow is Saturday and you don't have to go out. You hang up your wet coat and scarf and take a quick thumb-through of the mail before you change into something more comfortable: American Express bill, telephone bill, a solicitation from your college fund-raising campaign, a credit-card company's offer to lend $5,000, no questions asked, the bill from the plumber who fixed the leak yesterday, catalogs from Pottery Barn, Hammacher Schlemmer, Charles Keath, out, out, out, and then, placed directly underneath the Horchow catalog, there they are: the spring gardening catalogs.

With longing gazes, you stare at those glossy beguiling covers and already feel better, much better. The assurance at the bottom of the covers — "Satisfaction Guaranteed" — hardly seems necessary. You turn the pages, every now and then, wiping a little drool from the corner of your mouth, ogling masses of hardy carnations, each as perfect as a boutonniere snatched from a groom's tuxedo; hosta with leaves washed, waxed, and polished to green perfection; bearded iris, whose subtle spring-grape fragrance seems to waft up from the page as if from a perfume advertisement; ferns transplanted from some rain forest where dinosaurs still wander; tulips in wild, wonderful vibrating colors as if hand-painted by van Gogh; dazzling bouquets of peonies as delicious as rainbow sherbet; hyacinths, masses of hyacinths you could bury your face in (careful always, though, with those hyacinths, as it was a hyacinth analogy that landed Oscar Wilde in jail). Page by page you paw through, imagining how each plant will look in your garden and what sort of relationship you will have with it, the close-ups of dewy, creamy, smooth tulips as innocent as a sweet sixteen, others with a graceful, demure, aristocratic bearing promising seasons of luxurious splendor, others boldly flaunting their knockout looks. Which do you like the best? Why, tonight you like them all and will order them all — your own plant harem.

How many times in real life have you seen a model? Have you ever seen a model shopping at the mall? Has one ever sat next to you on a plane? Do you pass them on busy city streets or catch glimpses of them at trendy restaurants? Of course not. And the plant and flower models you see in these catalogs are just as likely to make an appearance in your garden. On such a night — and this is what the plant pornographers count on — your eyes don't see the makeup, the implants, the dye, the wigs, you're not even vaguely aware of the lifts, the tucks, the liposuction, the collagen implants, the petal augmentation, you don't know that these high-maintenance plants are working out at the gym four nights a week and slurping down Miracle-Gro shakes and injecting steroids. Nor do any of the tricks of lighting and photography disturb your misty thoughts. Such gardens of Eden, which have you so enchanted and entranced, truly exist only in the pages of plant pornography, and, in the minds of gardeners.

But the promises, all those promises, what of the promises?

The age-old promises are all there in the descriptions beneath the photos, enough to arouse a gardener's prurient interest and awaken springtimes of possibilities — "a continuous parade of luxurious summer color"; "hardy"; "mildew-free"; "strong stems"; "summer-long garden beauty"; "forty-three blossoms on each stem"; "return with renewed vigor each year" — all those wonderful old oxymoronic promises: "perennial tulips," "drought-resistant," "four-season petunias," "shade-tolerant," "continuous bloom," "white marigolds," "blue roses." It's the kind of night when the promise

"Yeah, sure, I'll respect you in the morning" sounds like a solemn eternal commitment memorialized in marble; you have no reason to doubt it. You want to believe. If it were any other night, you would remember how long your Stella de Oro lilies really bloom, or don't, each year. But your mind has blocked out the reality of flabby flower thighs and pimply plant backs, and you make a notation to order two dozen more, no, make that three dozen, to fill in that back border with a continuous parade of summer color.

Tonight your warm, fuzzy feelings extend beyond the flowers and plants to all the sick fantasy devices displayed in these pages. A trowel is a trowel is a trowel, Gertrude Stein may have said, but this is the sort of night when a $38 trowel with a hand-carved mahogany handle and a blade forged in Tuscany seems to make a lot of sense as the tool you've needed to plant properly; a night when a set of three trowels of different sizes for digging holes for different-size plants make even more sense; a night when French-enamel wheelbarrows and English-copper watering cans strike you as not only practical necessities but sensuous words of art; when you can picture yourself next spring on an Oriental kneeling stool, easing out weeds with your new carbon-steel hand weeder and tossing them into your Egyptian woven weeding basket. It is a night when everything Martha Stewart does suddenly makes eminent sense, and you know that next spring you'll finally have the time to undertake a lot of her projects. In fact, you may well want to press some of your more interesting weeds with a hardwood flower press and preserve them in collages or glue them onto lamp shades.

Seasoned gardeners know from experience not to place their orders on such a stormy night. No, better to spend some quality time with the catalogs tomorrow in the sunroom on the loveseat next to the shelf of Christmas cactus and geranium cuttings, studying the pages as the afternoon sunlight moves below the catalog along your legs and melts across the floor. It's good to be in when it's too cold to be outside and the wind sweeps through the hemlocks and bare branches of the oaks and moves the sunlight on the floor, to savor the catalogs and smell the moist potting soil and the greenness of the geranium leaves next to you and envision your own garden of Eden.

The winter might come quickly, and soon it's too dark to read. You gather the catalogs and secrete them in case anyone stops by.

Out the back window, through tops of trees, the small cold sun has already fallen below the tangle of branches, leaving behind colors like narrow bands of frozen ices, orange and lemon and raspberry, a line of blackberry extending farther out, and then the blue and purple and black of night. After dinner you go outside, crunching through the glazed crust of snow, to visualize the best site for a bed of Asiatic lilies. Snow drifts surrounded the fishpond, but the deicer has kept the water open, and beneath the surface the goldfish doze around the heating element. The night wind pummels the cold through trousers and coat, ski cap and gloves. The branches of the old oaks creak and clack in the frozen silence, complaining about winter.

Later, in bed, sleepy, you put the catalogs on the nightstand and turn out the light and listen to the wind pounding the north corner of the house, whiffling around the window frame, and you pull the heavy woolen blankets closer around you, and close your eyes while wind waves surge against the house in the night and tulips, luscious as lollipops, dance in your dreams.

IX
OUR LUCKY DAY

I REMEMBER AS IF IT WAS YESTERDAY our first visit to Kingsland Manor.

It was one of those chilly dreary misty late Fall days on the Cape when everything is shades of sodden gray and it seems like it has been this way always and will be this way forever, the kind of bleak day that makes you think of Dickens' "implacable November weather", of Melville's "damp, drizzly November in my soul".

We — my parents, my sister and I — had spent the long afternoon stopping at every antique shop along Route 6A, years ago the Cape's Antique Alley.

"There's one," someone would call out and we'd swerve into the driveway and once again be disappointed, finding once again what looked like the contents of an attic strewn about. It was getting late, we were getting tired, we hadn't bought a thing and mutiny was in the air.

"No more," someone grumbled; "I cannot go into another one. This is ridiculous. I'm sick of this."

A hissy fit seemed imminent.

And then, ahead, through the November gloaming, something caught our eye. Three lit globes atop a column. A sign: "Kingsland Manor Antiques."

"Stop!"

Amid ominous groans, we pulled in front of the shop. Outside, set in the manicured grounds around the house — for this, like many, turned out to be an old Cape house converted to an antique shop — were several impressive pieces of statuary. A large lion rested beside the front door, watching. We entered.

"*This*…is your lucky day," the jovial proprietor greeted us. "I'm in a *very* good mood. Today, *everything* is fifteen percent off."

Now in those days on the Cape, if a store hadn't sold something by November, it was stuck with it at least until Memorial Day. A ragged, wind-whipped seagull was just about the only living thing you would see for months. So, in retrospect, this, no doubt, was a last ditch effort to move merchandise. But that didn't cross our minds. He may just as well have told us everything was free. The hunt was on.

If all the other shops that day looked like they were filled with attic debris, this one looked like the owner was an accomplished cat burglar who had lifted the best of the best from old Palm Beach, East Hampton and Newport estates, and brazenly displayed the goods throughout his shop.

It was bright, well lit. Every lamp for sale was turned on, every piece of furniture polished, the silver gleaming, clocks ticking, the brass shining, fountains bubbling. There was an abundance, an overabundance, of everything. A display case filled just with Victorian bone-handled magnifying glasses and letter openers. Another with opera glasses. Another with battalions of lead soldiers. Everywhere were English bachelor chests, French bureaus, desks of inlaid tulip wood and kingswood; a graceful pair of bronze whippets, priced at $25,000, lounging on a prayer rug atop a Renaissance Revival library table; ebonized walking sticks with carved ivory handles; heavy silver trays; carved walnut medieval architectural pieces; sets of leather bound books; Tiffany bronze cigar boxes; Chinese porcelain fish bowls; Rose Mandarin garden seats; crystal chandeliers marked as coming from an Austrian palace; an Anglo-Indian ivory inlaid ebony desk; hand-painted Limoges bowls; walls of door knockers. There were pieces to shock: a huge oil painting of a voluptuous reclining nude; a marble putti fountain with a stream of water flowing from its penis; a stool made out of an elephant's foot. Two huge rooms of fabulous plunder.

When we had made the circuit and, dazed, dazzled, were back where we started, Norman winked.

"See anything you like? There's more."

More? He pointed to a passageway leading to a door.

Outside was a brick courtyard filled with garden urns and whimsical statuary, recumbent hounds and matched marble sea serpents, garden benches, a Victorian cast iron garden urn on a figured pedestal, and, under an old, gnarled tree, a garden pool where fat old goldfish leisurely swam. The courtyard was bordered by the ell of the house and by two outbuildings, an old barn and a garage, each filled with larger pieces: an Italian Renaissance-style glazed carved walnut bookcase, a complete Victorian-era saloon bar of mahogany, ready to be installed in your own mansion, stained glass windows, gold framed Continental paintings.

Norman was a man content, someone whose work was his pleasure, his passion. *Kingsland Manor* was his domain, his clubhouse. And he was lord of the manor.

He was probably in his mid-sixties when we first met him that late afternoon in November, affable, good humored. Wearing, always, a well pressed Oxford button down blue shirt, chinos and loafers with no socks, he sat in any easy chair by the front door, smoking his pipe and greeting the customers as they entered.

Bit by bit, over many subsequent visits, we heard his story. He had pulled up roots in Nutley, New Jersey, gave up his corporate job, and moved his family to the Cape where he had bought this old house which was set on a couple of acres on the Cape's historic winding Route 6A, and had set up shop. In the winter, he took his wife and son to Florida and had developed sources there for his inventory, buying more at the Cape's two nearby auction houses. For someone with a good eye and the time, there were bargains to be had there, especially in off-season auctions when there was little competition for unrecognized treasures. He would bring back his purchases, clean them up, mark them up and sit back and wait. It was a winning formula and he was making a fortune which he plowed back into more inventory, ever more expensive merchandise.

A wonderful life, a wonderful place to putter around, to sit and wait for those driving by to stop, to meet customers from all over the country, to work with his helper, George, who was like a second son, and with "my little Korean girl" who was actually from Taiwan and kept the flowers and grounds looking as if there was to be a photo shoot that day, who dusted and polished and looked after all of the rooms. No time clock to punch for Norman, no time sheets to hand in, no rat-faced boss, no services to perform for critical, complaining clients. Just come on in and buy it, if you like, otherwise thanks for stopping by. Truly he was one of those blessed individuals Winston Churchill called "fortune's favored children". "For them," Churchill wrote, "the working hours are never long enough. Every day is a holiday and ordinary holidays, when they come, are begrudged as an enforced interruption in an absorbing vocation."

Norman knew he had it made and reveled in his life, in this world he had created. And for his visitors, his customers, he had created an entertainment destination, with eye popping treasures and with him as the master of ceremonies. Everyone came back for more.

Norman could do stand-up with the best of them and wove his routines into wherever the conversation led.

"I work my tail off all day," he'd say, shaking his head and wiping his brow and trying hard to look as if it had been a grueling day, though he always looked like he had just stepped out of an ad for a Caribbean resort. "I go home exhausted, dead tired, walk in the door and you know the first thing Doris says to me? Norman! she says; Where are you taking me to dinner?"

He would shake his head in amazement. "Can you imagine? What has she been doing all day? Bridge? The beauty parlor? What a life. But every day it's the same: "Norman: where are you taking me for dinner?"

If his audience was receptive, he'd go on. "I'm not a picky eater. If she'd cook anything, I'd eat it. When I was in the Army, I thought that was the best food ever. No kidding. I'd ask for seconds. Give me more of that. SOS? I loved it. You know what SOS is? Chipped beef on a slice of toast. Shit on a shingle we called it. Me? I'd go for more. Doris? She doesn't think anything's good unless it's expensive. If it costs a lot, she likes it."

George, who had a real appreciation of the antiques Norman had amassed, as part of his job played the role of straight man. Norman would call for him: "Georgy? Can you bring over the yard stick?" Sometimes Georgy became Joey, sometimes Sammy, they had their own language, their own routine.

"Georgy, he's a good boy," Norman would say when George was out of earshot. "I couldn't do this without him."

Each antique store has its own look, its own flavor, its own specialty. Norman's focus was on the unusual, the unexpected, that singular piece that would rivet your attention.

In the mirror hanging in my hall — the one surrounded by an elaborate wooden carved frame of a howling grotesque — I can still see Norman seated in his chair, puffing on his pipe, sipping an iced tea. In the small silk prayer rug I have on top of a library table in the den, and in the English Renaissance carved heads I mounted on each side of the two wooden valances; in the small architectural pieces from an Indian temple; the high backed chair with turned arms and legs from the reception hall of a late nineteenth century mansion; the oak newel post from the mansion's staircase, the one with a woman's face and swags of garlands carved on both sides; the rosewood Chinese altar table two other customers wanted to buy from me as George and I were lugging it out to my car; the large Chinese silk panel woven with fantastic birds amid flowers and vines, mounted in a carved teak frame ("there's a tiny tear in that one section," George said and pointed it out, "but it doesn't detract from this piece. Please don't ask Norman about it or he'll have me take out a sewing machine and try to repair it"): in each of his antiques, now in my house, is a part of Norman.

Near the end, Norman was grooming his son to take over the business. But what Norman brought to his shop was a special eye, a special touch, a special genius for the work, that was one of a kind. It wasn't long after his death that the *Skinner* auction house auctioned off the remaining contents of *Kingsland Manor*, and the building was sold, once again to become a home.

And so it was that the antique shops along the Cape's Antique Alley, and the individuals like Norman who cherished them, one by one disappeared forever.

X
BUBS

Bubs, my elderly great aunt Margaret, had been in a nursing home for months, almost a year, when my parents got the call from the police in Toms River, New Jersey, that her modest, tiny bungalow had been burglarized.

Bubs was a spinster, "old maids" my grandfather, her brother, called these "spare aunts" who seemed to populate families in those days, a fifth grade school teacher who late in her career had been sent on her way when she became just a little too batty. There were the eccentricities that among ourselves we chuckled over, but Aunt Bubs always struck me as a gracious, genteel sort of lady, proud, very proud, of her membership in the Daughters of the British Empire, someone who aspired to be something more than she was, someone who came to spend more time than was healthy in her fantasy world.

She was one of five children born in the late nineteenth century to Christian missionaries in India (hence the Daughters of the British Empire connection), one of three sisters, each of whom fell in love with the same man, Dr. C. Burns Craig, a handsome, prominent neurosurgeon in New York City. Of the three sisters, Burns married Martha, and together they set about filling their home at 10 Gracie Square, one of the most exclusive addresses in the City at that time — the 1920s — with museum quality antiques they discovered in the many galleries in the City and at auctions at Anderson Galleries, the forerunner of Parke-Bernet and then Sothebys. Burns died of a sudden cancer when he was in his fifties, and Martha married again, to a wealthy ophthalmologist, and continued her collecting, until, on a vacation trip through the Great Smokies, their car skidded on a patch of ice and landed in a tree at the bottom of a ravine, killing her husband and leaving Martha in severe arthritic pain for the rest of her life. She moved to Florida to seek a healthier climate and, in down-sizing, her two sisters Edith and Bubs, and my mother, her favorite niece, became the recipients of everything she couldn't take with her. When Martha died, Bubs and Edith immediately set off together on a road trip to Florida, to grieve their deceased sister and to pack their car with every bit of loot they could jam in, putting aside until they returned to New Jersey the decisions of which piece should be kept by which of them, a Middle East-worthy conflict which flared and simmered for years.

We never saw much of Bubs. When the spirit moved her, she would join us for Thanksgiving or Christmas dinner, and on rare oc-casions stop by unexpectedly to bring my sister and me some relics from her teaching days, a box filled with jars of India ink long since dried to dust, a shopping bag packed with the loose unlabeled leaves and wood samples of a fifth grade science project. She never invited us, her sister Edith, or anyone for that matter, to come visit her. No one ever had been inside her home. So when the call came from the Toms River police, we were in the car speeding down the Garden State Parkway, at last to see what family heirlooms she had secreted.

We unlocked the kitchen door of the bungalow with all the an-ticipation of Howard Carter and Lord Carnarvon on that Novem-ber day in 1922 when they stood at the foot of the uncovered stone steps in Egypt's Valley of the Kings that led to the entrance of Tut-ankhamen's tomb.

Lord Carnarvon asked Carter "can you see anything?" as Carter peered inside, and Carter responded with words which became im-mortal: "Yes, wonderful things."

We were as stunned as Carter when we turned the key and swung open the kitchen door, but those were not the exact words we uttered. For it was obvious at once that Bubs was: a hoarder.

The kitchen overflowed with stuff. There's no other word to describe the detritus that covered all the counters, the sink overflowed with stuff, it was piled high on the floor, how could she have even used the kitchen, we wondered. The kitchen looked like a public health fire hazard poster, as did the dark narrow passageway to the two small bedrooms and to the living room, where cumbersome ancient floor lamps, with brittle, cracked electric cords, seemed ready to spark the inevitable fire. Even the shower stall in the bathroom was used as a storage bin, filled to the brim.

What had the burglar taken? Who would know? In that setting the greatest treasures of the Louvre and the Metropolitan would not have stood out as anything special.

The pane of glass was missing where the burglar had smashed it to turn the lock and raise the window between the living room and the front screened porch. Upon entry he was, no doubt, as stymied as were we, and anything easily turned into cash — silver, jewelry, electronics — was as safe in this chaos as if locked away in Fort Knox.

"Let's at least take these lions," I suggested after we had secured the house, pointing out the pair of white marble British lions I had spotted in the shower stall, their heads emerging out of piles of newspapers and old shopping bags filled with whatever.

"No," my father said; "we don't know when Bubs is getting out; we don't want her coming back home and finding things missing. That would really push her over the edge."

My mother and I argued, quite persuasively, that it was unlikely she would ever be able to leave the nursing home and live by herself, that even if she did, she wouldn't miss anything in this jumble, and that even if she did, we deserved something for helping out — it was my father she would call at two o'clock in the morning when she was convinced her blouse buttons had been bugged, asking him to call the F.B.I. — and that even if we hadn't helped her as much as we could have, we were her sole heirs, so all Martha's antiques should stay in the family. And that family would be us. But my father's righteous high road prevailed that day, and my mother and I left empty-handed, feeling not unlike a frustrated rapist.

Within a week, the police called again. The house had been broken into again.

This was a call to arms.

"OK," my mother and I said in unison, "we have to go down there right away and get *everything* out."

"You can't," my father said, already distancing himself from this adventure with the use of the word "you" rather than "we". "You have no right to do that. She's still alive. Those are her things."

When it became clear he would have no part of this mission and was looking at us as if thinking "do I even know these white trash grifters?", we tried to enlist the assistance of my sister who happened to be visiting that weekend.

"No way," she lectured us. "I think what you are doing is just wrong. I am not going to be any part of it."

So, like young Jim Hawkins and his mother returning to the Admiral Benbow that frosty night in *Treasure Island* when all the town folk refused to go back with them for fear of pirates, we set off alone, to claim what was rightfully ours.

It was cold, a very cold, sunless winter's day. We were bundled in heavy coats, ski caps, scarves, gloves. There was no heat in the bungalow. The propane tank was empty. And the water, too, had been shut off. We would have to be back on the road home long before nightfall. All of which meant that, like Jim Hawkins and his mother, we had but several hours to do our work.

Where there's a will there is indeed a way and what followed must have looked much like that old, television game show where the winning contestants had a certain number of minutes in a store to grab whatever they wanted.

We pawed through every drawer, every closet, every cabinet. One bureau drawer was filled with nothing but cardboard toilet paper rolls, another jammed with empty Quaker Oats containers. We learned then that we had to check everything, for inside two of those Quaker Oats cylinders, wrapped in faded tissue paper, were exquisite etched glass Lalique vases.

There, its sensuous wood glistening even in a dark dingy corner, was what, in family lore, was called "Martha's French chest", said to be from Marie Antoinette's Petit Trianon. Are you kidding me? We had to have it! But how could my mother, over seventy, and I, get it into our station wagon without help?

How we cursed and ridiculed the Simon Pures at home that day. But we did it. It was like one of those incredible news stories you read about when a child is pinned under a car and the parent is able to raise the car several inches to pull out the infant. We looked at this chest of drawers. We stroked it. And the power surged. We emptied the drawers onto the floor, checking the chaotic piles and picking out a perfect chunk of petrified wood, a fern fossil, several arrowheads with a handwritten note they had been found on *Tempest Farm*, my mother's family's ancestral farm in Liggonere Valley, Pennsylvania. We carried the drawers outside one by one, the easy part, and then, manhandling the chest out and onto its back into the station wagon, inserted each drawer back in, and shoved the chest in as far as it could go.

Time to lower the back seat of the station wagon because Martha's dragon table we had long coveted must come home with us too, a black teak three legged China Trade table with a fabulous ferocious carved dragon twisting up the base, and a circular opening in the top for a piece of Rose Medallion to be inserted, which miraculously, we found in another room, wrapped tightly in brown paper and string, and, even more miraculously, undamaged. The large ornately decorated Imari umbrella stand would fit in next to it. My marble lions from the shower stall were set on the floor of the front seat, no problem that they would be banging into the legs of the passenger all the way home: whatever sacrifices were required would be made — without complaint.

Ours was a deep search. An old alligatored buffet had two locked doors. I had brought with me a bag filled with miscellaneous keys for just such a contingency, and tried one after another. Bingo! Inside, behind stacks of old papers, wrapped in yellowing newspaper, were a pair of black cloisonné vases, inlaid with the Imperial dragon with its five turquoise blue toes, a momento from our missionary forebears years of service in China in the late 1800's. A very delicate carved ivory box. A small spinach jade box. A brass candlestick from India shaped like a hissing coiled serpent. Circular Persian trays of brass inlaid with fantastic designs wrought in copper and silver.

Deep in the buffet was a pile of old used envelopes, folded again and again into lumps and bound with dried rubber bands which split without so much as a snap when we pulled them off, each envelope holding a ring, a brooch, a pendant. Without taking time to assess their value, into our gathering gunny sacks they were plopped. Under chairs, under Burn's writing desk, were Oriental rugs rolled up and bound in brown paper and tied with cords. Homeward bound they would go. We tore through a linen closet filled with bath towels, so worn they wouldn't be used to polish a car, disgusting dusty stacks of them, and almost closed that closet door when we felt something beneath them. And pulled. Out emerged an enormous, filigreed sterling silver serving tray.

Which raised again our on-going question of the day.

One of the main issues in the Middle East-worthy conflict between the two elderly sisters was who should keep Martha's silver. It was the Gaza Strip of their warfare. It was not as if either of them had any use for a nineteenth century formal English silver set. Edith did no entertaining except for an occasional bridge group lunch, and no one ever had been invited to enter Bubs' home, let alone to come for lunch or dinner or tea. Yet the possession of Martha's silver had become a matter of principle. We had heard enough of this conflict, from both sides, to know that Bubs currently had possession of the silver. How this had happened was a matter of debate: whether Martha once had told her she could have all the silver, or whether she had simply taken it, under the theory that possession is nine-tenths of the law. But if Bubs had it, it was certainly eluding us, and we concluded, bitterly, that the burglar had found the silver cache, and how foolish had been those who advised us not to take anything after the first break-in. And that was that.

What's going to happen to Bubs' car?" I asked, as the dark winter afternoon grew deeper. It was an old Chevrolet, sitting under the carport on the side of the house.

"I think I saw the keys in the kitchen," my mother said. "Should we see if it even starts? Shouldn't someone be driving it every once in a while?"

Neither of us wanted to mess around with the car; taking it out for a spin was asking for trouble and we knew if we had to call for help, we'd have a heap of explaining as to who we were, and why we were there, and why our station wagon was packed solid and exactly what we were doing emptying this house of a poor old spinster in a nursing home. We did unlock the front door of the Chevy and looked in, pushing aside a tangle of old black umbrellas and ladies' rubbers, then opened the trunk and with the tips of our fingers, moved aside a stack of filthy burlap bags.

And there, underneath, was the fabled treasure: grocery bags filled with Martha's silver. Coffee pots and tea pots. Trays. Covered vegetable dishes. Creamers. Sugars. Fabulous sets of sterling silver dinner plates and small dessert plates. Heavy ornate candlesticks and candelabra. Bags bursting with monogramed flatware. We took them all, forcing them into every nook and cranny left in the back of the station wagon, and when there were none, or the spaces were too small, pushing and shoving, manhandling in the precious bags.

We stepped back and slowly, inch by inch, so that nothing broke, pushed the back door shut.

The car was riding lower. Much lower. And there was nary a crack for the driver to look out the back window.

What if we're pulled over for that violation?

OK, let's get our story straight. Exactly what are we doing with all this, this — loot? Where have we been? Where are we going? Just what's going on here?

We went over our story until we had ironed out most of the kinks and worked up a plausible alibi, which rose or fell, in large measure, on a look of mother/son innocence we would have to muster and maintain under intense cross examination. We knew for sure that whoever answered our one phone call home for help would give the cops all the information they needed to book us for grand larceny, with no hope for one red cent of bail money.

Like a golden retriever you've left home alone which makes a point of ignoring you when you finally return, we received no cheerful greetings and no offers of assistance in unloading the station wagon when at last the weary pickers returned. And no one showed the least bit of interest in looking at the plunder which we proudly displayed in the living room to admire. "I just think it's wrong," my sister would mumble as my mother and I once again were rehashing with glee the details of our exploits.

Just as it took years for Howard Carter to excavate and explore and recover everything in King Tut's tomb, so it was with our discoveries. It wasn't long after our trip that Bubs passed away in the nursing home. We knew enough by then to hire some off-duty firemen with a U-Haul to go to her bungalow. We met them there, and watched as they loaded everything into the U-Haul — from Uncle

Burns' mahogany writing desk to the locked steamer trunks that were in the crawl space above the living room, all of which they then unloaded into piles in my parents' garage and my garage.

At the end of *Treasure Island*, Jim Hawkins, put to work sorting the hoard of pirate coins and packing them into bread-bags, reflected: "I think I never had more pleasure than in sorting them", even though "my back ached with stooping and my fingers with sorting them out." Such was our pleasure in pawing through the hoards in our garages.

This was dirty, filthy work. We had to wear rubber gloves, and, from breathing dust and dirt and ancient mouse droppings, had to take frequent fresh air breaks to blow out black mucus from our nostrils, and every stitch of clothing had to be washed after each session. There were many false leads — old locked steamer trunks which sent visions of sugar plums dancing in our heads, until we broke the locks open with a hatchet and found nothing but stacks of old sheets almost petrified into each other. Or flannel blankets we in disgust pushed into plastic garbage bags and sealed tightly. Or yellowed lace curtains and stained linens. Or stacks of crumbled newspapers.

But shiny nuggets glistening here and there in the dirt and dust kept us dreaming and ready to resume work each day. A wonderful Chinese fisherman carved of mellow old ivory. Sets of Tiffany china with bands of cobalt and outer rims of gold. Elegant glassware. A butter churn from *Tempest Farm*. A wonderfully carved boxwood figure of one of the eight Chinese Daoist immortals, riding a dragon. A tall mirror framed in polished yew with a nineteenth century maritime oil painting set near the top. Trunks of old family hand-sewn quilts. Soapstone carvings of Chinese idols. A brass inlaid incense burner. The *Tempest Farm* dinner bell. A family of elephants carved of ebony. Books from the early nineteenth century and late eighteenth century. Old oil paintings waiting to be identified. Elaborately carved Oriental frames inlaid with ivory. Old Chinese silk table runners. An enormous brass key that looked like it was from a medieval monastery. Small Indian brass bells that once had circled an elephant's neck.

To clean and restore these pieces, and then to assimilate everything into our homes, would take time. And it would sometimes be months, sometimes years, before we really examined, and fully appreciated, what we had. But always we were grateful that Bubs had cared enough about family history to preserve these bits and pieces.

On a strip of adhesive tape on the bottom of a small fragile piece of Belleek, Bubs had written: "Grandmother carried on horseback over the mountains", and on the bottom of another piece of old Staffordshire she had taped a faded note that read: "Dear Burns, this saucer is from the China set given to your grandmother Craig when she married in 1828. Mother, December 1930". Without such identifications from the past, these would just be pieces of china, of no particular interest or value. Now, identified and properly displayed, they, for us, rivalled pieces of Captain Flint's legendary pirate treasure hoard.

With the disordered, chaotic, tattered, yellowing piles of personal papers we took away, one fine day we came across a carbon copy of the "Last Will and Testament of Martha White Craig Frost" dated December 24, 1949, about twelve years before Martha died, which proved to be a veritable Rosetta stone to the loot we had liberated. Just as in *To Kill A Mockingbird* everyone's repeated references to an old "chiffarobe" almost gives that piece of furniture a presence in the novel, so the will named certain pieces that had, through the Homeric oral tradition, become a part of our family history.

"The antique music box" my grandmother was to receive, which was never found, had become the subject of endless speculation — over what had happened to it, who had taken it, what it had looked like, whether anyone remembered it from visits to Martha's Gracie

Square home, its value (which, over years of speculation, increased until we were sure it must have ranked right up there with the greatest music box ever made). There was a black sheep stepson who was left but $100 under the will, who knows, the family history went, what he had taken, maybe the music box? There was the "French glass and enamel clock" which went to Edith and some years later was stolen when her small second cottage at the Jersey shore — which she had purchased specifically to house what she had inherited, and took, from her sister's estate — was burglarized. "Two small French bookcases brass mounted" which went missing. "My ship model" which my grandfather had always admired — a handsome model of the clipper ship, *Flying Cloud,* Burns had purchased at auction. The jade "cuff-links from Cartier" which we called "Burns' jade cuff links". The "solitaire diamond ring and the diamond band from Cartier given me by my first husband, Dr. C. Burns Craig" which the executor of Martha's estate sent to my mother by regular mail, uninsured.

To Martha's sister, Edith, "three Hopkinson Smith water-colors". Bubs had penciled in under this clause on her copy of the will — "2 located" — and in fact Edith did have these two which she proudly had hanging in her living room: a sun-drenched French countryside landscape with haystacks, and the other, a dreamy languid river-side scene along a back water of the Marne. (On the back of this one, Burns had handwritten a note which he dated July 4, 1921: "I greatly admired this painting of the Marne by F. Hopkinson Smith and Miss French, authoress, and friend of Mr. Smith, gave me the picture as a token of gratitude for real or fancied aid which I had given to her during a year of illness", signed C. Burns Craig, to which he added a note: "In Aug. 1918 I crossed the Marne at Chateau Thierny with 77th Division".)

(F. Hopkinson Smith, I learned, was a true Renaissance man. Born in 1838, a descendant of one of the signers of the Declaration of Independence, he was an accomplished engineer, designing such public projects as the foundation for the Statue of Liberty; he was a prolific and best-selling author; and he was an artist of renown, the leader of a small group of artist friends which included William Merrit Chase and Winslow Homer. Smith's plein air watercolors, pastels and oil landscapes, had a feel similar to Chase's and Homer's, a realism trending toward impressionism. He was collected at the time by such patrons as John Jacob Astor and Isabella Stewart Gardner, and his paintings are now in many public collections including the Museum of Fine Arts and the National Museum of American Art.)

After helping my great Aunt Edith one summer with some landscaping work at her shore house, she took her two F. Hopkinson Smiths off the wall, and insisted, against my protestations, (mild to be sure), that I take them home with me.

Two Hopkinson Smiths that had never been to market! Straight from the artist to his good friend, Miss French, to my great uncle, Dr. Craig, to Martha to Edith to me! But that tantalizing reference in the will to a third. What happened to it?

Amid the pile of dust-covered prints, lithographs, mezzotints, some loose, some in old frames, beneath some faded prints of fashionable French ladies in delicate gold frames now sullied with layers of grime, there lay a watercolor, a scene looking straight into a forest of trees, with streaks of sunlight through the trees illuminating the landscape. I had learned early on always to have a magnifying glass at hand, and running it along the bottom of the painting, taking a rag and pushing aside the dust that clouded the glass over this painting, was that familiar signature "F. Hopkinson Smith"! Bubs hadn't even realized that it was right there in her house, buried in a pile of attic debris. And whatever the burglars had stolen paled when compared to this one dusty painting. At last, as Martha had hoped, her three Hopkinson Smiths were together.

In just such circuitous ways do pieces that long have been together seemed to exert some strange gravitational pull on each other, so that all of Martha's antiques we liberated now complement each other, once again, as they were at 10 Gracie Square. Or, is it that some of us — like Bubs, like me — feel that same inexorable pull to preserve, to hold together, bits and pieces of our families, those few tangible remnants of our own connections to the misty past?

XI
I SAY A LITTLE PRAYER

TREASURE DOESN'T ALWAYS TAKE THE FORM we expect. While we're searching for a glistening cache of gold doubloons and moidores and fistfuls of pieces-of-eight, when we're hoping to happen upon an unrecognized Tiffany peony lamp, or a Townsend eighteenth century mahogany tea table with those open talons grasping ball feet, or for that toy soldier made in the Russian workshop of Carl Fabrege, as we look for the mother lode, real treasures sit unnoticed in plain sight. And there is no treasure map leading us to them.

Once, when cleaning out a deceased relative's home to get it ready to put on the market, at the end of a long, dirty, dusty day, I began filling shipping bags with old books from the bookcase in the spare bedroom. No time to try to determine what was what, which might be a rare first edition; I just stacked them — the oldest looking ones — into brown paper bags and loaded them in the car to take home.

Years later, with a friend who is a computer whiz, I had begun selling a few of these old books on eBay, and success with some led me down to the bookcase in the basement where I had stored them. There was a bunch of books on the shelf which all looked the same. They had almost grown together into one indistinguishable moldy, musty old mass, covers missing, discolored, water stained. One, upon inspection, was a Bible with a date in the front of 1782. The leather or sheep skin binding was worn and dry and flaking, all the pages were brown and stained, some were torn, some pages were unbound, and it was a candidate to be thrown out with the trash. But in an amateur's mind, old equals valuable, so, with a few others, I gave it to my friend to list on eBay just to see what happened.

She began doing research on the internet about each of these books before posting them and started uncovering tantalizing clues about this Bible which stoked our dreams of a treasure island, including finding references to a Bible of the same date that was valued at over $100,000; but we quickly brought ourselves down to earth, knowing at least how tiny differences can make big differences in value.

A buyer of one of our previous listings — a 1797 House of Representatives Journal — had emailed and asked if we had any other offerings coming up, and my friend wrote back to him about the Bible. He was knowledgeable, honest and generous enough to suggest that it sounded like we possibly could have an Aitken Bible, and that we should be cautious with it, that it potentially was very valuable, that we should recognize this and be careful not to let it go for less than it was worth. He was interested, he said, in purchasing this book; he easily could have dangled a thousand dollars before us, which we would have swallowed, hook, line and sinker, but instead he wanted us to know the background of the book and began emailing us information — how the Aitken Bible of 1782 was the first Bible ever printed in the United States, how the Bible was published by a Philadelphia printer, Robert Aitken, after it was reviewed and approved and authorized by Congress, and how copies of this very rare, historic text had been valued at as much as $195,000, with one held in the collection of the Morgan Library. There had been facsimiles made of the Aitken Bible, but if mine was a fake, the fakers had gone way overboard in aging it.

Clearly, we were holding something that was above our pay scale to identify and evaluate, so, after making an appointment for a Saturday morning, we wrapped it carefully in tissue paper, placed it in a shoe box, and brought it to the rare book department at Sotheby's.

There a specialist sat down with us, took one quick glance at the remains, and instantly shook his head sadly.

"No," he said gently, as if he knew what he was talking about, "I'm afraid we won't be able to accept this. It doesn't meet our minimum value for an auction". And he laid it back to rest in the shoe box and shoved it toward us.

"What is your minimum?" we asked in wide-eyed amazement and innocence.

"Well," he said, "to even be listed in one of our auctions, the book would have to be expected to bring over $6,000, and I'm afraid this simply would not." He pushed the shoebox closer to us.

"But, but, we've seen these on the internet with an appraised value of well over $100,000."

He smiled wanly, shook his head sympathetically. "Yes, but those would be examples in much better condition than, than… this."

The shoebox had now been maneuvered right against our fingertips.

He stood up and put out his hand to usher us out the door so that more important collectors could receive an audience.

"But we do thank you for your interest in Sotheby's," he added as he herded us out of his office.

"Yeah, right," we said as the elevator door closed. "Wait till he sees how Christie's snaps it up!"

We high-fived.

It may as well have been his twin brother working in the rare book department of Christie's. Or maybe Mr. Sotheby had run over and gotten there a few minutes before we did to hand over the same script to his counterpart. Because the response was word-for-word identical, including the patented sad looks and the gentle shove of our sorry little shoebox.

We left discouraged, dejected, deflated.

"Well, those are the experts."

"Maybe let's just put it on eBay and go with whatever happens."

"But remember our friend who advised us to be careful?"

"I know, but what does he know compared to The Experts at Christie's and Sotheby's? They know what they're doing."

"Okay, let's go back to New Jersey and think about it for a week before we do anything else."

So, rather than a celebration lunch at the 21 Club as we had planned, we grabbed a Subway sandwich and left the City.

Re-grouping, licking our wounds, a few days later I remembered Swann Galleries, a smaller auction house in New York City which specializes in manuscripts, posters, photographs, works of art on paper, old master drawings, specialty books — what is sometimes all lumped together as "ephemera". Was it worth a shot? One more trip into the City on a winter's weekend? Okay, why not.

This time was different. When the expert at Swann's watched as we opened the shoebox and unwrapped the Bible, his eyes danced. We heard a, "Wow" as he held it, reverentially, then an, "Oh my God", and then a more judicious, "This is very very rare" — exactly the words we had been waiting to hear.

"Where did you get this?" he asked.

I explained that my great-grandfather had been a missionary and minister and had had a collection of Bibles, and that this had been among them.

"Is this something you could include in an auction?" we asked tentatively, afraid of what would come next.

"We would *love* to include this. Have you shown it to any other houses?"

We had rehearsed our story enough to lie and say no, wanting him to think he was our first stop, that our book was not shop worn, that it had not already been turned down twice by the big boys.

"Can we sign a contract today?" he asked. "Or is this something you'd want to go home and think about?"

Every fiber of our being was screaming, "How much? How

much?" Until one of us casually asked, as if it was the last thing on our minds. "What would your estimate be on this?"

"So, just an educated guess, of course, and it depends, as you can imagine, on many variables" — how much, how much, our eyes screamed as he continued his cautionary prelude, blah, blah, blah — and then, at last, "but my best judgment is that this book, in this condition," and here he laid out all the problems with it which we could see, "would go for around $10,000."

Ten thousand dollars was not $100,000 and was certainly not $195,000, but $10,000 was a lot more than just an old book sitting in a damp basement, deteriorating, so on the spot we signed the contract for the book to be included in the next auction of *Printed and Manuscript Americana*, to be held in two months.

He had noted that there were thought to be fewer than 100 copies of this historic book in existence, but Swann's excitement with our discovery of one of those fewer than 100 did not extend to featuring the Bible on its catalog cover. Or even to a mention of it in its pre-auction brochure, which featured highlights of the coming auction.

Fast forward through two months of sweet dreams. That morning of the auction, for the first time, the reality of what an auction is set in.

You need someone out there with a consuming interest in an Aitken Bible, something we hadn't even known existed, had never even heard of, until a few months ago. You need that person to have a burning desire to acquire an Aitken Bible. You need that person to have the wherewithal to purchase an Aitken Bible, and to have that wherewithal on the day of the auction. You need someone who has somehow learned that an Aitken Bible is coming for auction today, at this auction. You need someone with the time today to devote to this, today.

How improbable would it be to have all those conditions converge?

It gets even harder. A lot harder. You don't just need one such someone. You need at least two such someones to make an auction.

You begin to think about the probabilities of winning the lottery. Isn't this just about the same? Expect nothing, then you won't be disappointed.

The minutes of the auction morning pass slowly, endlessly, until, at last, our lot comes up at 10:40 a.m.

The auctioneer opens the bidding at $7,500, below the suggested low of the range in the catalog, which had been listed as "$8,000/$12,000". All we need is one person to bid that amount and we're ready to celebrate at 21. Three seconds pass, which feel like three hours, until at last some intrepid soul jumps in at $8,000.

It's like being underwater. Time stands still. Reality is suspended. You are an observer, looking up through the pool at the gauzy figures standing around whose mouths are forming words you can't hear. You wait for another bidder to commit.

One Mississippi.

Solar systems collide.

Two Mississippi.

Ice ages come and retreat.

Three Mississippi.

Civilizations rise and fall.

Four Mississippi.

The outer limits of eternity are revealed.

You are listening for, "Going once, going twice", when instead you hear, or think you hear through the water: $8,500!

Two second later it's $9,000!

Now we have out two someones. Now we have an auction!

One second later $9,500!

Then after two long seconds more its $10,000!

Ten thousand dollars. Swann's prediction of what our book would bring. A logical pausing point when the bidders must be thinking: "What the heck am I doing? It's clear I'm not going to get this on the cheap. Do I really really want this moldy old book?"

Three seconds to ponder these questions and the bid, suddenly, is now $11,000!

Up now in increments of $1,000. Each second another bid. Each second another thousand bucks. Straight up to $20,000.

Time again for the bidders to think. $20,000?

At this point you are silently yelling at the bidders. "Come on! Be a man! It's just money! Don't wimp out! Go for it! Grow a pair!"

A full five seconds before the bid jumps: $24,000!

Now we're going up in increments of $2,000!

Fly me to the moon! Yes! Come on, suckers, fly me to $100,000! Over $100,000! There are less than 100 of these Bibles. In existence!

Five seconds now between each bid. They are thinking harder. Don't think! Act! This is a once in a lifetime opportunity! Bid!

Five seconds. Five seconds and we're up to $39,000!

Six seconds between bids now. They are getting weary. You can feel it. Come on! Come on guys. It's just money! You know you want it!

Less than two minutes after the bidding began — how can that be? — at least two hours elapsed — the bid of $46,000 hung out there with no one else jumping in.

Sold at $46,000!

And it's on immediately to the next lot as you realize you've been holding your breath. Inhale. Resume breathing. Look around, touch things to ascertain if those two seconds had been a dream or really happened. From a drenched shirt, you know either you had the night sweats or it really was real.

The old moldering book that had sat for years, unnoticed, in an unused bedroom in a tiny bungalow in Toms River, New Jersey, had just been translated into $46,000 cash. A moldering Bible from my great grandfather's collection.

No doubt about it, there is still treasure out there, out there in the most improbable spots, waiting to be discovered. And always will be.

XII
MAKING A STATEMENT

THEY WERE AN ELDERLY COUPLE, all the way from Virginia, Barbara and Ted, both short, neatly dressed — Ted in tie and tweed jacket, Barbara dressed for a ladies formal luncheon, this at a time when most of the other dealers were in T-shirts and sweatpants — polite, reserved, sometimes one or the other dozing, seated on the metal folding chairs in front of their booth at the Morristown Armory.

The Armory, with its threatening olive green World War II tank aimed at the road out by the entrance, and its cavernous echoing militant space and cracked concrete floor, was just about as inhospitable a venue for an antique show as could be imagined, but over the years, as the traditional shows that had been an annual tradition for twenty-five years, forty years, sixty years, fell by the wayside, the Morristown Armory twice a year filled the void, and all the dealers from up and down the East Coast, who wanted to exhibit, came here.

Barbara and Ted were of a different world, a hold-over from the golden age of shows. When Barbara saw you were interested in one of her pieces — she specialized in very fine China Trade antiques — she came alive, talking about it, showing why it warranted its price, always weaving in stories from her half century in the business. She seemed as happy telling her tales to a new, receptive audience as she was selling something from her display, while Ted played the role of obedient husband and let his wife hold center stage.

The first piece I bought from Barbara was a twenty-six inch Famille Rose palace vase. Yes, it was calling to me, to be placed at the entrance to my living room, but at that time I was unsure of antique Chinese porcelain, not certain whether this one was real or a modern day knock-off of the kind you might find in one of those mall stores peddling "Orientalia". It was expensive so I had to be sure.

Dealers at a show must be evaluated and judged on the spot, just like a lawyer picking a jury must make a multitude of instantaneous judgments about a prospective juror. Is this someone who knows what they're talking about? Is this a person I can trust? Barbara passed with flying colors. She went over every inch of the palace vase to demonstrate its authenticity and age, early 1800s, explaining the meaning of the colorful scenes of Chinese men and women, flowers, birds, butterflies and mythical creatures, the stories behind the scenes, and what the gilt foo dogs and dragons which graced the vase represented. Ted was there to wrap it, carefully circling the vase with layers of *Depends* and duct tape, and insisting on carrying the swathed bundle out to my car, parked far away in the muddy rutted lot around the Armory.

Now I was no longer just a customer; I now was a new friend. And at the next Morristown show, Barbara and Ted greeted me, eager to tell a new story, to show off a new find or something they thought I might like, this time a pair of Rose Medallion temple jars.

"These will really make a statement," Barbara said. She already knew me too well. How could I resist those words? Sold! Whether or not they have ever made a statement to anyone but me? I'm not sure. But on either side of the mantle above my living room fireplace, they speak distinctly each time I pass.

At other shows, I had to convince her I was worthy of something in her exhibit I saw and wanted — a large pair of bronze Chinese fern bowls, embedded around the outside with koi in full relief.

"Are you sure you can use these?" she asked skeptically. "Do you have a place for them? You realize how heavy they are?"

Yes! Yes! And yes! By now I was salivating. Reverse psychology? Maybe, maybe not. I tend to think not. Barbara may have been a very adept salesperson, but her real happiness did seem to come in placing one of her children — she called her antiques her "children" — with someone who seemed truly to appreciate it. Ted positioned these heavy bronze bowls on a dolly and slowly began wheeling them through the Armory.

"What *are* those" another dealer joked with him as he passed by, "spittoons?"

We knew better and continued our procession to the parking lot, happy that these ancient treasures from the Far East were going to a caring new home.

Over the years, I sometimes would let them know of something I would like, something for them to look for in their travels. I had tried that with other dealers and never heard from them again. With Barbara and Ted it could take a while, but they always came through. A Famille Rose fenestrated chestnut basket with under tray. A Rose Medallion planter with saucer, a combination particularly hard to find.

At one of the shows, I had asked if they might be able to find one more palace vase. They promised they would keep an eye out for one.

"Still looking," they would tell me when I walked up to their booth months later at the next show, reading the question in my eyes even before I said hello. "We haven't forgotten."

And then one day, Barbara called, the first time we had spoken by phone. She was excited.

"I have them! I found your palace vases!"

Them? Vases? The mission was to find one palace vase. The thought of two hit me right in that spot where it hurts, the spot where that deep dull pain is localized when you realize you may have to spend money you hadn't planned on spending at that time. And didn't have.

"I knew eventually, if I kept looking, I'd find them," she continued. "This is truly rare: a pair! Perfect condition! Both of them!"

I was mentally prepared to purchase one. I had the spot picked where it would go. But two? Barbara could read my hesitancy.

"I'm going to have Ted take some photographs and send them to you. He'll mail them to you today. Or tomorrow. Probably today. You will love these. I have never found a perfect matched pair before in my fifty years in the business. This is a first for me."

True to her word, the photos were in my mailbox several days later. They were *Polaroids* and the colors didn't seem quite right, there was a turquoise tone which made me question the age of the vases. I would tell Barbara at the next show, would thank her very much indeed for tracking them down, but tell her that they didn't seem right for me.

She called a few days later.

"Did you receive the photographs?" she asked.

I thanked her and started to tell her how the colors weren't exactly what I was looking for, that they didn't seem quite right.

She knew more about what I was talking about than I did.

"Oh, they're right," she said. "They are exactly right. These are early nineteenth century, late eighteenth perhaps. There is no question about that. Ted and I will drive them up so that you can see them. You have to actually see — with your own eyes — something like this, to appreciate just how special they are."

"That'll be great," I said. "I'll see you at the show in May."

"Oh, no," she said, "you can't wait that long. We'll drive them up this week. May we stop in on Thursday? Just for a few minutes?"

"I couldn't have you drive all the way here from Virginia," I said, starting to feel boxed in and beginning to back-pedal and sweat a little. "At the May show, next month, that'll be fine."

"We insist," she said. "This is what we do for our best customers."

"It's too long a trip," I protested. "Just the next time you have to be in New Jersey we can — "

"Nonsense," she said. "We love to travel. It's our only excuse for getting out of the house. Otherwise we just sit around all day looking at each other. Do you think I enjoy that?"

Now I was feeling trapped. Having them travel over four hundred miles? Just for me? Showing me pieces they prized, that they had tracked down. Just for me? What do you say? There they are. In your house. Gee folks, I really don't like these? Now get back in your car and drive four hundred miles back home?

"Of course you have no obligation to purchase these," Barbara said, again reading my thoughts. "If for any reason. But I said to Ted, I know these will be perfect for you. These are just what you've been looking for. Someone with your eye will truly appreciate the exceptional quality of these. Would there be time to stop in before you go to work? Or would the evening be better? Or we can even come to your office."

That was not a sight I relished: a tiny elderly couple lugging two palace vases through the office? Suddenly, a visit to my home seemed to be making more sense, though I was still trying all the diversionary tactics I could muster: I leave early for work. Very busy schedule. Don't get home until late in the evening. Nothing worked. They would arrive at my house at 7:00 a.m. that Thursday morning. Did you need directions, I asked, worried about them driving through the maze of suburban roads in a day before the advent of navigation systems.

"Oh, no," Barbara assured me, "we do pretty well at finding anything."

At precisely 7:00 a.m. that appointed morning, not a minute before, not a minute after, their minivan pulled into my driveway. I went out to greet them. Both were as fresh and energized as if they had just downed a quart of *Red Bull*. Ted already was hauling two boxes out of the rear of the van.

"Let me help you," I offered, grabbing onto the end of one of the boxes.

"No thank you," he said, asserting control over the box. "I know what I'm doing; it's better if I do it, in case something goes wrong."

"Would you like to use the bathroom?" I asked when they were in the house.

"No, no thank you," they both said. "We're fine."

"Let me get you something to eat. Something to drink." I had all possible breakfast foods ready for them.

"Oh no, thank you; we've already eaten."

Ted was now on his hands and knees on the living room floor, pulling a swaddled palace vase from its box, then unwrapping it.

He stood it up.

And it was perfect.

"It looks so much better than in the photographs," I said, amazed at how beautiful it was. "The colors, I hadn't been sure, but they're just right."

"See, I told you your photos are no good," Barbara joked with her husband. "You really have to see an antique, to look it over, to be able to judge it. These are very special. Ted, show him the other."

Ted paused, rolled his eyes and looked at his wife as if to say "I'm doing this just as fast as I can," then unbundled its mate and stood it next to the first: two perfectly matched palace vases, early 1800s, in my house.

"Where are you thinking of putting them?" Barbara asked, looking around. "These could go in so many different spots."

"I was thinking there," I said, pointing into the dining room, "on either side of the Chinese altar table."

"Oh, yes, yes," Barbara said. "Ted, let's try them there."

They each took one and set it down by the table. Barbara stood back, then adjusted Ted's vase just a fraction of an inch.

And it was good.

Again, offers of food and drink and bathroom. No, they had to be on their way. I showed them where I had placed their temple jars on the mantelpiece, the Chinese bronze fern bowls in the front bay window on tall taborets, each overflowing with a huge spider plant, the chestnut bowl in the kitchen. They were pleased, but wouldn't linger. They would not impose.

"We know you have to get off to work."

"To make money to buy some more of your things," I joked.

They smiled. "Well, we hope we can find some more pieces you'll love. We're headed up on a New England gathering trip right now. We know just where to look."

Barbara knew how to whet a customer's appetite.

"Go for it!" I said. "Have a great trip. Happy hunting. Bring it all to the next show."

"We will," Barbara said. "This may be our last trip up here, our last show. We keep saying that, I know. But we're both well into our eighties now and . . . Well, we're going to keep doing this just as long as the good Lord will let us."

In their eighties? I was stunned.

They were in their van and going down the driveway before 7:30, as I went back into the house to admire my new acquisitions before going to work.

I saw them at the next show in May, but then, at the October show, the spot where their booth always had been was occupied by another dealer. I asked the dealer at the adjoining booth and learned that Ted had died. And a year or so later got that news of Barbara's death.

In his book, *Treasure Hunt*, about the growth of the famous Israel Sack antique business, Harold Sack tells the story of his father receiving a call in the 1930s — the fearful start of the Great Depression — from a Connecticut picker who had found a very rare New York Queen Anne marble top tea table dating from about 1740-1750. Excited about this exceptional discovery, Israel Sack called one of his best customers, Henry du Pont, to offer it to him.

"Sorry," said Mr. du Pont, "but I have no money to buy with at this time, Mr. Sack, and I've deferred all purchases for a while."

Sack was so convinced that such an important piece deserved to be part of a great collection that he persisted. "Let us bring it down and show it to you," he suggested to a reluctant Mr. du Pont. Once it was in du Pont's home in Delaware, he found the money to pay for it, and it of course was there forever. It now graces the fabled Winterthur collection. Israel Sack was so happy to find just the right home for this rarity that he took only a tiny profit on the transaction.

It's wonderful when that happens, when you can develop that sort of relationship with a dealer, when the world comes to you. Over the years, through various shows, I came to know another husband and wife team of dealers, from Maine, who developed a sixth sense of what would appeal to me. Sometimes they would bring something to a show and not exhibit it until they had a chance to show me first; other times, between shows, they would write and send photographs of something they just had found; and once they kept me informed about a piece they hoped someday to acquire. An old friend in Maine, they told me, had a large, dome-topped China Trade carved camphor wood chest, the likes of which they had never encountered before. Their hope was to purchase it from their friend when she broke up her house to go into an assisted living facility. For several years they mentioned it now and then and asked if I might be interested. It was certainly something I wanted to see, and when at last they acquired it, they let me know right away. The measurements, alas, were a little too big for me, and try as I might, like Cinderella's step-sisters trying to force on the glass slipper, I had to concede that it was not a piece I could use. But it seemed just right for my parents' house on the Cape, and they were interested. The dealers drove three hundred miles to their home, looked around, placed it where they thought it would look best — where it remains to this day — joined my parents for lunch and were on their way.

If you find the right dealer and can size them up and are comfortable putting your trust and faith in them, they may well know more about what is best for you than you do yourself, and be justified in pushing you toward it. And they can be an extra set of expert eyes, scouring secret nooks and crannies around the country for treasures for you.

A lovely couple, Barbara and Ted, they were unique, those rare dealers who became your friends, who knew just which pieces would appeal to you, who never pushed unless they were certain they were right and you needed a push in that direction. I would look back, time and again, throughout the years, each time I walked by one of their "children", and be thankful, always, they had made sure I saw the same light they saw.

XIII
PLAYING HOOKEY

IN MY LAW PRACTICE, I was representing an arbitrageur, a professional speculator who took positions in stocks when rumors floated that one publicly traded company might take over another. When such rumors began to bubble about any New Jersey company, my mission was to feed him information, to find out as much as I could about the situation and to relay this intelligence to him the instant I learned it. I was not told what position he was taking to better keep my analysis unbiased. Such assignments are inherently challenging. One is dependent on sources developed over the years — on friends in the industry, in the agencies which regulate companies, on lobbyists and lawyers who have represented similar companies or been regulators — anyone who may have insights or their ears to the ground and could feed you scraps of information which, taken in isolation, may have meant nothing, but with a few other scraps, and your intuition thrown in, begin to paint a picture.

All was going well, my network of contacts was helpful, I felt I was getting solid information to my client; all was going well until . . . the day the judge handling aspects of the matter announced that he was holding a special closed door session the following afternoon at 1:00 p.m. with mandatory attendance by all counsel. Something was up, but what? All counsel clearly did not include me, but I decided I at least should be outside the courtroom to grab whoever I could the minute the doors opened and, like a dog, begin begging for table scraps.

It was mid-July, the kind of sweltering day which can be a New Jersey summer specialty, when I drove down to Trenton in the shimmering heat haze and began pacing outside the courtroom as the various counsel gathered and gossiped and I pretended I wasn't eavesdropping. At exactly one p.m. the courtroom doors opened and I found myself — maybe as a result of the heat — doing something I had not planned or contemplated. I walked into that courtroom. Trying to hide amid the group of lawyers filing in, I took a seat behind a tall, linebacker of a lawyer, opened my empty decoy file folder, leaned over it, looked at my blank legal pad and began busily scribbling nonsense as the gravity of what I had just done began to sink in and wet saddle bags grew under my armpits.

I could hear the judge opening by saying, "YOU! Yes you! In the second row! Who are you? Stand up! And wondered what the penalties might be for contempt of court. A fine which would exceed my legal fee? Mandatory jail time?

The judge entered, we rose, he sat, we sat, and he began the proceedings, announcing his rulings on ancillary pending matters as I leaned closer and closer into my legal pad and wrote down every word he uttered. When the thrust of his rulings was clear, I fought every impulse to rush out and call my client; I was stuck now, until everyone left, even though I now knew everything I needed. When the judge adjourned, I was in the midst of the clump of attorneys moving out the door, pulling out my cell phone and reaching my client before anyone else learned the news.

Whether or not my timely report helped my client in any way I had no idea, but I had done my job, creatively and professionally, with, I thought, cunning and a heavy dose of daring, and, satisfied by a good day's work, got in my car.

It was only 1:35 p.m. There certainly seemed no need to drive back to the office on a steamy summer afternoon and work on yet another case, did there? It was not hard to convince myself I deserved a break after that half hour's hard labor. I made my way straight to Princeton, to the coolness of the Nassau Inn set back from the main street, its history dating back to 1756, and downstairs to the quiet of the Tap Room for a glass of iced tea. Before heading home, a victory lap, as it were, around Palmer Square seemed in order.

There is nothing as wonderful as a southern town — and Princeton certainly qualifies — on a hot summer afternoon when everyone with any sense is away, or inside, and time hangs suspended. I leisurely poked around the little empty shops. Wallowing in the luxuriousness of unexpected freedom, of nothing at all that had to be done.

In the window of the Silver Shop — that quaint, tiny old store that had been in business there, in that location, since 1937, carrying a line of estate silver, jewelry, porcelain, crystal and glass — in the window, certainly placed there to entrap me, was a deep cobalt blue dessert plate with a wide scalloped gold border and a white center surrounded by gold.

Should I?

Or shouldn't I?

Should I?

Or shouldn't I?

I really don't need any dessert plates. Lead me not into temptation.

But don't I deserve some sort of reward for what I just did today? I can at least take a look, can't I? There will be something wrong with them, the price will be way out of my league, and I'll move on and go home.

It's easy to convince yourself of anything on a sultry summer afternoon after scoring an improbable touchdown.

I open the door, the little bell rings to announce my entrance, and I casually inquire about the plate in the window. It turns out to be part of a set of ten. Limoges, France, late 1800s, each in pristine condition. No nicks, no rim chips, the cobalt, the gold, as pure, as deep, as rich, as the day they were hand-painted. The price not unreasonable, and a request for a "best price" makes it just a touch more reasonable. Within moments they were mine and I was walking out with a carefully held bag, back into that hot Princeton summer afternoon. In due course, the client would pay his bill, but I never would learn whether my information had assisted his speculation. No matter. The plates were all the reward I needed. And I never forgot the sense of joy to be absent without leave on a midsummer afternoon.

There would be many more business trips that took me to Trenton, always with stops at the Nassau Inn to replay that magic afternoon, with visits to the Silver Shop, where, through years of changing stock, nothing else ever caught my fancy. Which I took to be a positive sign of good mental health; that I was not a compulsive buyer. (There was, of course, the *Gilded Lion*, a block or two away, an antique shop that could have been the model for Dickens' *Old Curiosity Shop*, but that is another story of temptation for another time). Nothing in the Silver Shop that is, until many years later when, I happened to have a half hour after lunch at the Nassau Inn before heading to Trenton and ambled around Palmer Square. There, in the window of the Silver Shop, was a sign: 'RETIREMENT SALE'. This of course was meant as a personal invitation. To me. To come in.

A young clerk standing in for the owner told me that after all those years, the owner was retiring, and yes, the Shop would close forever, and, by the way, everything in the Shop was now 40% off the marked price. And the sale had just started the day before. Clearly the young clerk was adept at antique foreplay.

Time now for a careful final look around, I went over each shelf in the small shop several times, visualizing where I could use each piece that momentarily caught my eye. Nothing called out as a keeper, nothing, but in the search for antiques there are many more dry wells than gushers.

I was ready to head out the door when, to say something to the clerk before leaving, I mentioned the bronze tiger crouching on the counter. Now in many shops in Princeton, there are all sorts of tigers, the mascot of the University, and I've inquired many times in other shops and have always been told, "Oh no, that's not for sale; that's just for display." I had seen no price tag on this tiger so was sure that was the case.

"Oh, it's for sale," the clerk said and showed me the tiny price tag hidden on its underbelly. I quickly did a 40% reduction calculation, the price still high, but the tiger was staring at me, burning bright. I started asking the clerk questions about it to give myself some time to think and weigh the pros and cons and consider where I might put it.

"You'll have to ask the owner," he said. "He'll be back later this afternoon. All I know is that he told me it was old. And I noticed some sort of Oriental marking underneath."

I picked up the tiger, satisfyingly solid and heavy, and there, underneath on its belly, were a few Chinese characters, which of course meant nothing to me but clearly were calling out — "Old. Chinese. Buy me!"

Without showing any excitement and before he worried and decided to wait for the owner to return, I helped him calculate the 40% discount, paid, and carried my tiger back out to Palmer Square and onward to its new home: atop a bookcase, standing on an antique Chinese silk runner, backed by a brass tray inlaid with dragons, and lit by an old soapstone lamp in the form of an elderly Chinese priest.

Isn't it funny how the few times playing hookey are the moments we remember in delicious detail and cherish most of all?

XIV
THE LAST DAY OF SCHOOL

CLOSING DOORS IS WHAT I ALWAYS START THINKING about on a June day like this. A day when you can almost taste long, lovely kisses in the air. The sort of day that always reminds me of our last days in high school.

Do you remember those days of enchantment? In your eighteenth Spring? Can you hear it? In a song from our soundtrack of that year? The songs all of us listened to on a transistor radio? That captured everything we were feeling then, almost deciphering everything in our lives we couldn't quite understand? Remember?

June, then, was full of such days of enchantment. I remember those leafy green mornings, sitting in darkened classrooms with the overhead lights turned off to keep the rooms cooler, the doors along the hall open for cross-ventilation, the venetian blinds, drawn against the sun, billowing slowly in a hot breeze and then slapping back against the open windows. I remember the drone of a lawn mower moving back and forth across the far playing fields, and the green smell of June grass, and girls in summer-print shifts and leather sandals.

It's something about June days. I'll be driving along some street, and the way the branches of the oaks arch over the road and intertwine will remind me of Druid Hill, where Haven lived. Or I'll be daydreaming and start to hear in the leaves moving with the breeze the rhythm of Joanna's voice, the rise and fall of it, her intonations, and then, quite distinctly, fragments of our conversations, and pretty soon the three of us will be talking. About the things we talked about as we drove under the twining oaks, past the green lawns and houses set back from the road. Into those honeysuckle mornings.

Those were days of long lasts looks, of looking at the people you had been with most of your life, really looking at them, with the sudden realization that you might not see them for ten years, or twenty, or maybe ever again. You looked at them as if you had never seen them before. Which you hadn't. The nerds. The hunks. The preppies. The hippies. The students. The studs. The introverts. The extroverts. The surfers. The jocks. The friends. The enemies. The perky cheerleaders. The pot heads. The faceless ones whose names you never knew, whom you had never spoken to, or heard speaking, each one, you now realized, someone special you wish you had known. The leaders and losers. What would become of them? "I can't look at everything hard enough," Emily said to her mother at the end of *Our Town*. Looking — suddenly you saw them, the uniqueness of each, and loved them all.

One period after another, the classes ended.

The students changed rooms and walked down the halls.

Walked down halls airy with those sweet June breezes, into the crowds.

And were gone forever.

And then, the quiet of June descended, like a benediction.

There is no place as peaceful as a school a few days after graduation, as hushed as a Civil War battlefield, the parking lot empty, the windows shut, the blinds all pulled to the same level. The banner that all month had been over the entrance to the gym — SENIORS RULE — gone. Walking around the outside of the building and down to the playing fields, you feel like a veteran trying to recall just what the sides had been, and why.

Under the trees, shadows drift on the grass while sleepy summer insects drone overhead. As you sit in the shade, you know that although they all now are gone, everything here will always be the same. On those blue-sky afternoons of September, Coach will be out on the field barking orders to the football team. The track team will be running laps. All year long, after school, students will be putting together the newspaper, the yearbook, rehearsing the play. The band will be practicing. Miss Johnson will be tutoring her students in the chemistry lab. And each June there will be several students who spend their study halls outside, in the sun, in love, who do not want it to end.

Mornings, green mornings when time stopped at Thoreau's "meeting of two eternities, the past and future, which is precisely the present moment," driving to school on those leafy green mornings when the branches of the trees arched over the roads and we rode on waves of music and June's dappled light.

XV
THE FIRST DAY OF COLLEGE

THAT PARTICULAR SCAB SEEMED PERMANENT, having healed nicely over the gaping, bloody wound from years ago.

Until this week.

When good friends reported that they had just taken their youngest son to college. And showed me a photograph. There they were in his dorm room. Momma Bear and Papa Bear looking drawn and exhausted but game to put on a happy face, and Baby Bear, whose expression was inscrutable slash sullen. They reported that on the drive to college, Baby Bear had reminded them — apparently more than once — perhaps *warned* them was closer to the reality — not to speak to anyone, ANYONE, when in the dorm. And if perchance they were spoken to, to respond, but not with a joke. They seemed to have understood this directive and to have abided by it, recognizing that their role — they who had made this day possible — was fully captured under their designations: Sherpa One and Sherpa Two.

My friends were feeling a bit dejected about it all, and I'm sure were thinking of Momma Rose's line in her song in "*Gypsy*" when her kids split: "One quick look and out with the garbage."

"What is wrong with us?" they asked me: "are we that repulsive?" Hardly. Of any adults, my friends were supremely presentable: Momma Bear was very attractive, (any 18 year old boy would have had sweet repetitive dreams of doing her), and Papa Bear was a very successful businessman (who was a master at relating to young people). Why was Baby Bear so embarrassed?

I assured them it was not them, that this was a Universal. And, watching blood ooze out from around my now dislodged scab, told them my story.

OK, so the day came at last when I was off to college.

The ride from home to the campus in our Station Wagon jammed with all my belongings was three hours door to door, enough time to issue marching orders to my parents: their role — I said this with utmost diplomacy — was to help get everything deposited in my room, and that was it: to then turn tail and get the hell back in the car and depart; not to help me unpack anything; not to talk with anyone; not to look around; not to return to my room: essentially, to get the job done and then to floor it out of there. Of course there were the to-be-expected rejoinders: are you embarrassed of your parents; we'd love to meet your new friends; let's look around the campus so we get a sense of where you'll be, after all . . . . But certainly by the second hour of the trip I felt confident that they both understood the importance of these directives — to me — and would at least humor me and abide by them.

Which gave me time yet again, to ponder the real troublesome elephant in the room, that looming, disquieting matter of: a roommate.

Remember that scene in the first chapter of *Treasure Island* where the old Captain, staying at the Admiral Benbow Inn, tells young Jim Hawkins he would pay him a silver fourpenny on the first of every month to keep his "weather-eye open for a seafaring man with one leg"?

How that personage haunted my dreams, I need scarcely tell you. On stormy nights, when the wind shook the four corners of the house and the surf roared along the cove and up the cliffs, I would see him in a thousand forms and with a thousand diabolical expressions. Now the leg would be cut off at the knee, now at the hip: now he was a monstrous kind of creature who had never had but the one leg, and that in the middle of his body. To see him leap and run and pursue me over hedge and ditch was the worst of nightmares. And altogether I paid pretty dear for my monthly fourpenny piece, in the shape of these abominable fancies.

My abominable fancies of who my roommate would be occupied not just my nightmares, but repeated random moments through each day and every day.

He of course would be a mouth breather, blasting halitosis into our cell-like room all night long, just several feet away from my head. And he would have a troublesome impacted clump of snot lodged in one nostril that would rattle up and down his nose all night, sounding like a sick cat outside our window. Until, with one enormous death-rattle like snore, it was launched out the nostril and, with unerring accuracy, would plop onto my pillow, inches from my face. And the smell! The smell in our room would be enough to knock you out and have you cracking the window even when the winter winds howled outside, a curious mixture of bad breath and B.O., and that stale smell of soiled sheets and dirty clothes, of sweat slickened socks cast about the floor, and ragged pee-stained underwear with tire tracks, turned inside out to dry out and ripen over the back of his desk chair. All mingled with the dominant order of wet farts, which ripped out with Big Ben like regularity.

I'd look up from my studies, highlighting pertinent passages of some indecipherable tome, to see him gathering the ingredients for his personal Thanksgiving: his index finger deep in his left ear, twisting, probing, digging, easing out what looks like a helping of turnips. He sniffs it, and it must have been smelled good because he then eats it with apparent relish. Next on the menu must have been creamed onions because the same digit is probing for some up his nostril. At last, success, and he extracts it, smells it, then rolls it around, again and again, between his thumb and first two fingers. He attempts to flick it off, but it doesn't dislodge, so he sticks it underneath the seat of his chair, apparently to save for a later time, when needed. It must be grooming day because now he's taken off his socks — has he ever changed them?—and is working on his gnarly toenails, clipping them and brushing the clippings onto *our* rug, then taking the top of his ballpoint pen and using the edge to dig under his toenails to extract the festering masses of black debris deep under the nails, sniffing each extraction and then using the edge of the seat of his chair to dislodge them from the tip of the pen.

In *Moby Dick*, when Ishmael found there was no room at the *Spouter Inn* in New Bedford, and he would have to share a bed with a stranger, or, wander out into the stormy night, Melville wisely observed:

> No man prefers to sleep two in a bed. In fact, you would a good deal rather not sleep with your own brother. I don't know how it is, but people like to be private when they are sleeping. And when it comes to sleeping with an unknown stranger, in a strange inn, in a strange town, and the stranger is a harpooner, then your objections indefinitely multiply.

Melville recognized this universal truth one hundred years ago. What is it with colleges thinking that a mandatory roommate freshman year is a good idea?

My abominable fancies of course continued. And intensified.

I'd be sitting in my reading chair, trying to complete the impossible assignment of reading pages 183-327 of *Don Quixote* before the 9:00 a.m. class tomorrow, while my roomie sits in his chair, not six feet away, a magazine open on his lap, his trousers down to his knees as he struggles mightily to rub one out. "Love don't come easy," as Diana Ross sang it; ain't that the truth. With groaning and moaning that makes me consider calling for help, and then a shout as if he had scored a winning touchdown, and then a splat, as a gob of Guy Goop lands on Cervantes' masterpiece. That night, under the covers, he'd be back at work.

And speaking of under the covers, just as in *Moby Dick*, Ishmael's unwanted bedmate slept with his harpoon, I was pretty sure my roommate would be sleeping with a lacrosse stick or hockey stick.

The miles passed by. My roommate thoughts became more troubling.

When we at last pulled up in front of my dorm — which struck me then as being as forbidding as a correctional facility — my mind was focused solely on The Plan — somehow getting everything into my room, and then, somehow immediately getting my parents to take off. With the alacrity of bank robbers. In retrospect, I have no idea how we did it: three beasts of burden, climbing the three flights of concrete steps to my floor, as quiet as if on moccasined feet on a midnight raid of a colonial village.

Opening the door to my room, a burst of heavenly light, like sunlight pouring through a church's stained glass windows on Easter morning: Mirabile dictu! The arrangement was two separate rooms! A bed in each room, the rooms connected by an inner door, now closed. All my worries washed away in the first moment of the first day of my first year at college. Smooth sailing from now on. And then. . . .

There of course had to be an "and then", didn't there? No one escapes such watershed moments unscathed.

And then . . . as I was preparing to herd my parents out the door and on their way, a mysterious shopping bag appeared in my mother's hands. Where did it come from? I hadn't seen it.

I stared in disbelief as from it she extracted a yard stick. And then from the bottom: a pair of shears. And then a pencil. And then . . . a roll of shelf paper. And laid everything on the floor, then went to my bureau and wiggled out the top drawer and laid it on the floor, next to her equipment. Dumfounded, I watched as she unrolled the shelf paper, spread it in the drawer, and began taking measurements with the exacting precision of an ophthalmologist about to perform eye surgery.

I tried every entreaty, every threat, but I may just as well have been talking directly to the shelf paper. Nothing stopped her from her appointed task. I was sweating profusely, looking around to see where my father was. And as I did? Saw now, at my open door, all of the students from my floor, peering in, trying to fathom exactly what strange ritual was being performed.

What to do? What to do? Was it too late now to seek admission at another college? Obviously, my four years here were now over, my reputation ruined.

I stepped over to my father, looked him in the eye with a wide open psychotic stare which could have been the look of someone about to go postal, and in a soft — so no one else could hear — yet frighteningly firm voice — so he could understand the gravity of the circumstances — said, each word clipped: "I. Am. Begging. You: Make. Her. Stop."

I was sure he would understand my predicament and know just what to say to stop this madness. But instead, he shrugged his shoulders a little, sort of gave a wan smile like he had been through such situations many times before, and said "there is nothing I can do. Until she is finished."

OK, there were two parents there, time to make my wishes known. I stepped over to my mother as she measured, and hissed at her — quietly, but as threatening as a coiled rattlesnake — "I am Begging You. STOP. NOW!"

"Oh don't be silly," she said, not in the least bit concerned, "you don't' have to beg. You need shelf paper in every drawer. We have no idea what's been in these drawers."

OK, that just made it worse. The audience was moving deeper into my room to watch, sniggering, thinking of exactly what an adult might think had been in those drawers.

"This will just take a few minutes. If you don't bother me," my mother helpfully added.

OK. Cut loss. Don't engage her. It will only get worse. I had seen her in these types of situations before where there was no telling what might spill out of her mouth next. "Oh yes, Arthur was born with a very small penis, but we . . . "

Cut loss. Make it end.

The last drawer at last was returned to the bureau.

It was over. And so was any fantasy of passing myself off as one of the cool kids, that fantasy now on the floor amidst slivered scraps of shelf paper.

XVI
A KNOCK ON THE DOOR

IT ALL BEGAN JUST THE WAY GLORIA later would tell me all magical parts of our lives begin: there would be a knock on the door, the phone would ring, a letter would arrive. And just like that, our world would change forever.

My book, *Gardening in Eden*, had been published in 2003. I liked it, a lot, but had spent eighteen months trying to find a publisher who agreed with my favorable assessment. For a year and a half, the largest commercial publishing houses, to the pathetically puniest boutiques, had summarily rejected it with nary a scribbled "not bad" on one of their form rejection letters. And only then, after a year and a half of trying did I receive a phone call at the office from Michael Korda, the legendary editor-in-chief of Simon & Schuster, Simon & Schuster!, telling me he'd love to publish it. And would be my editor. In abject gratitude for his perspicacity, I dedicated the book to him. We received a glowing bouquet of blurbs for the dust jacket, but that was about it, for the book on publication fell flat on its face, with no reviews, and sales as anemic as a scraggly impatiens. Any friends who even referred to its existence invariably said that they were "not really into gardening" so had not read it — yet — though my book had about as much to do with how-to-garden as *Walden* had to do with how to construct a cabin in the woods.

So when I got home from work one day that Spring and found in the mail a letter from a reader saying how much my book had meant to her, I soaked up the praise as the parched soil around that scraggly impatiens would soak up the rain. And because that reader, and that letter writer, was Gloria Vanderbilt, I read it again and again, absorbing the nourishing rain through every pore.

I had never met Gloria, never corresponded with her, and, being from a different branch of the family, felt no connection to her. Here was one of the most iconic, recognized women of the twentieth century, writing to me, telling me about how much she enjoyed my book and, how much she would love to come see my garden.

About fifteen years before, I had written *Fortune's Children: The Fall of the House of Vanderbilt*, and a section of that book had dealt with the famous custody battle for ten year old Gloria Vanderbilt, a ferocious battle between two momma bears, her very young, globe-trotting mother, Gloria, and her very wealthy aunt, Gertrude Vanderbilt Whitney. Talk about a headline case: this custody battle and the trial in "Matter of Vanderbilt" were daily front page news in 1934 during those dark days of the Depression. Having read about her abhorrence to talking about her past, and her constant refusals to be interviewed about it, I had not even tried to reach out to her when I was researching and writing my book. Now, here was a character right from its pages, writing to me, saying how much she would like to come visit. It was as if Samuel Clemens answered his doorbell and saw Tom Sawyer standing right there, looking at him.

Of course I wrote back. I always answered each of the reader letters I received, which was not so hard to do since rare was the month when I received as many as one. And thanked her for her kind words and said I'd love to show her the garden, any time, believing that would be that.

By return mail, Gloria replied: when? when might be a convenient time?

Lord, was she serious about this? She was. As I read her reply and this began to sink in, I was sweating. Now, I've had a lot of fun with my garden and to me it is a work of art, but I was not quite so delusional that I believed it anything more than an amateur's effort, that someone like Gloria Vanderbilt had seen all the greatest gardens of the world, and what I had done on my shy half acre was not worth her time. I pictured her getting out of a stretch limo, taking one look at where she was, and saying "Oh …", the same sort of "Oh …" I had heard in every form rejection letter.

I responded with a date, sure her social calendar would be filled. Her response, "Perfect!", was in the return mail.

How do you transport a world-famous eighty-year old heiress from New York City into the wilds of New Jersey? I offered to line up a driver for her, sure she would say that Beasley would be driving her. (Beasley had been her mother's chauffeur before the child custody trial in the 1930s, so maybe it would be Beasley's son, or grandson, or a Beasley equivalent?) "That would be lovely" came her reply.

What do you do to prepare for the arrival of such a guest? You can be sure that in the remaining days every leaf in my garden was hand-polished, every blade of grass precision cut, every brick in the paths scrubbed. For a week, daily sacrifices and offerings were made to the weather gods that the big day would be sunny and fair.

And it was. As the hour approached, I had no idea what to expect, what to say. I visualized the arrival of a diva, bedecked in jewels. In truth, when the Lincoln Town car arrived and the driver opened the back door, out stepped Gloria, in a very simple cotton dress and straw hat and sandals, no tiara, no jewelry, not even a ring on a finger.

Here was one of the most famous women of her time, in the headlines since birth — first as a baby in a fabled family — at that time the richest in the world — then for the custody battle, later for her many affairs and four marriages, someone photographed at every opening night, at every charity event, perennially on the best dressed lists, famous for her Vanderbilt jeans, her television ads featuring her perfect butt and wispy WASPy voice, her perfumes, her fashion empire. And the first thing I blurted out was "Oh my God! Its Anderson Cooper's mother!"

She smiled. Her smile, like Gatsby's, had "a quality of eternal reassurance in it", but behind it she seemed as shy, as fragile, as Laura in *The Glass Menagerie*, as if it had taken as much courage for her to reach out to come visit a stranger as it did for me to welcome a celebrity into my home. She seemed so vulnerable that every instinct to protect her came to the fore.

She stood looking at me for a moment: "oh, yes," she said quietly. Though not a direct descendent in her family line, some of the Vanderbilt genes must be so dominant that I do bear a striking resemblance to many of her forebears whose portraits hang in *The Breakers*. That, and my mention that we shared the same birth date — February 20 — and it was as if we had known each other and been friends for life. We began calling each other "cousin".

I lead our tour out through the French doors in the sunroom to the terrace, and, babbling away, up the stone steps that lead to the garden paths, all the while silently praying that a neighbor wouldn't choose that moment to start mowing their lawn or using a cyclonic leaf blower. But all was quiet save the rustle of the new green leaves of the oaks and the chirping of happy birds, straight out of a Disney film, when I realized I had lost my tour. I looked back. Gloria was standing in front of the large green nineteenth century demijohn I had filled with water and placed on the brick wall around the terrace garden, standing back, pacing around it, examining it from every angle. I walked back to her.

"Enchanting," she whispered reverently, as if examining the Hope Diamond. "This is exquisite."

I explained that my grandmother had had it on top of the stone wall around her sunken garden in Maine and I had always been taken by the color, the way the sunlight passed through the green, illuminating it like a stained glass window.

"Enchanting," Gloria said again, and showed no signs of wanting to move on. She was committing it to memory, and I realized later she would have liked to have sketched it, to have sat right there and painted it, for she was looking at the world with an artist's eye and a child's sense of wonder, everything to her, even in this, her eightieth Spring, was new and fresh as if never seen before, as if this was the world's first day. This green bottle had enchanted me since the time I was a child, but this was the first time I had met anyone who had shared my fascination.

"There's more," I promised, trying to lure her onward. At the rate we were moving, it would be dark before we left for dinner.

Gloria was the kind of guest gardeners fantasize about as we're on our hands and knees trying to pry an impacted rock out of a hole to plant a hosta, or battling slugs and groundhogs, or nuking weeds, someone who sees our garden as we see it in our mind's eye, something that matches the images and fantasies in our dreams that we try, always unsuccessfully, to bring to life.

I led her along the brick paths, past drifts of Virginia bluebells and violets and Johnny Jump-Ups and Jack-in-the-Pulpits and red tulips, islands of hosta, moss and lichen covered statues of the four seasons looking so old that they may have been lifted from a Renaissance garden, a peek into the gazebo with its small glass-topped table and two chairs that would have been perfect for a Parisian café, to a hidden nook with a weathered teak bench surrounded by arbor vita and forsythia, with the oaks and ash towering over it.

"Oh, my" Gloria said, as if entering a fairytale forest. "Let's sit down here so that I may remember this."

We sat. And she put her hand in mine.

I was holding the hand that had held the hand of Marlon Brando. Of Howard Hughes. Of Frank Sinatra. Of Truman Capote. Of Bobby Short. Of Anderson Cooper. The thought of which might have been enough to turn my hand into a raging river of sweat. But with Gloria, we were transported into a Zen state, inhaling the green of Spring, listening to the music of birds, hearing what the rustle of the oak leaves above was trying to tell us. And it was a long time before either of us broke the silence of that dreamy afternoon.

Never before, or since, have I encountered anyone with such a deep appreciation of life, of being alive, of the miraculous wonder of the moment.

There was about an hour to kill before we would leave for dinner and now we sat in the sunroom, talking. Gloria assumed I knew all about her financial problems, which had been in the news some years before, but I didn't: the story of how, after the sudden death of her husband Wyatt Cooper at the age of fifty, and the suicide of her twenty-year old son Carter who fell to his death from her penthouse terrace as she implored him to stop, she had begun to see a psychiatrist, who, in her vulnerable state, eventually took financial advantage of her, having her sign over to him — unknowingly — the keys to her fashion empire, leaving her with enormous tax liabilities and no income. I gathered, in asking a few gentle questions, she was having serious trouble making ends meet, even on a monthly basis, it was that bad. I sensed she would never trouble her famous son, Anderson, with her problems.

We began brainstorming ideas for making a come-back in the fashion industry; she was game, but different avenues all seemed precluded by whatever she had signed. I then moved on, encouraging her to write a book. Some years before she had written two about her early years, *Once Upon a Time*, and *Black Knight, White Knight*, both of which had been well received and bestsellers. Why not one about her friendship with Truman Capote? She visibly cringed. "I would never do anything to keep his name alive," she hissed. And snarled. I knew that while they had been best friends, the friendship ended when he published *Answered Prayers* with its cruel depictions of Gloria and some of her friends, but I hadn't realized how deep her dislike of him still ran, decades later. OK, scratch that idea. How about portraits of some of the famous people she had known, and

I mentioned a handful. I could see her turning this idea over in her mind, and the fact that she didn't dismiss it summarily perhaps meant that it may have taken root.

I took her to dinner at nearby Baltusrol Golf Club where we sat at a corner table, looking out over the perfect green course and lovely pond as the evening darkened. There, Gloria did something I was to observe time and again: she all but vanished in front of my eyes, doing nothing to call attention to herself, melting into anonymity. As eager as my eyes were to dart about, flashing in neon a SOS: "Look Who is Sitting With Me!", I protected her privacy. Part way through the dinner, Bill, the bartender who had been there over fifty years and had met everyone, from the Duke of Windsor to Arnold Palmer to Dwight Eisenhower, came over and very quietly said "Good evening, Mrs. Vanderbilt" as if it was the most natural thing in the world, just the way Scout said "Hey Boo" in that final scene of *To Kill a Mockingbird*. And Gloria said hello as quietly, as shyly, as Boo.

When we finished dessert — by now we were laughing because we were finding how similar we were, we both had ordered the same appetizers, the same main course and for dessert rice pudding, our favorite — the driver I had arranged was at the front door to take Gloria back to the City. We embraced and waved goodbye. Which I assumed would be forever.

Except that when I awoke and checked my computer — we had exchanged email addresses — there was a note from Gloria that she had sent before dawn, thanking me for her garden tour, and then getting right to the point: "which of these do you like best as a title for my book?" listing three or four for the book she said she had decided to write about her "romances".

From that moment on, I was present at creation, with email ideas flying back and forth, often several times a day, and occasionally a draft chapter faxed to me for comments. Gloria was looking to me as her first reader, to offer ideas and criticisms, but her way of writing was so idiosyncratic, her experiences so other-worldly, that to change a word, or to try to re-arrange a thought, felt like disturbing a delicate, perfectly balanced mobile.

Opening the chapters Gloria was faxing to me was like opening treasure chests, never knowing what to expect, but always being dazzled, from her first affair with a prep school friend, to finding a Bible in Truman Capote's bathroom with the pages cut out to form a secret place to hid cocaine, to Howard Hughes flying her to Catalina, being chased around Bill Paleys penthouse in the *St. Regis*, sleeping with Marlon Brando who was "more more more everything than even I could have possibly imagined", how on the table next to his bed was a ten by twelve "drop-dead-gorgeous" photograph of Himself in a silver frame, Frank Sinatra singing *My Funny Valentine* to her, all wrapped around what it was like in those dreamlike days to be very young and very beautiful and very rich in old New York before the War.

Gloria titled her manuscript *It Seemed Important at the Time*. I was convinced it would be a bestseller, but, unsure of its merits, Gloria asked what to do next. I suggested she contact my editor, Michal Korda, who was pleased to publish her book at Simon and Schuster. Even then Gloria had little understanding of her celebrity status and how to use it to promote her book. "Get on Oprah." I advised, and when she replied "how would I do that?" as if that was the most impossible thing imaginable, I was dumbfounded, knowing how I would have milked that name recognition to promote one of my books. "Just call her and say you'd like to come on to discuss your new book, all about your affairs with Brando and Sinatra, and Hughes." She was too modest to pick up the phone or even to suggest this to her publisher's publicity department.

But she did receive invitations to appear here and there, one to come to a major book fair in Scottsdale, Arizona and to be a featured speaker there.

"Would you come with me?" she asked. She could bring one friend. Having all but guaranteed Gloria that her book would be a bestseller, I was happy to jump into the trenches with her. We planned our three day trip with military precision.

Gloria must have thought I was doing something important at the office because she never called me there, though of course it was my fervent hope that she would. And that I would not be at my desk. And that the receptionist would have to page me: "Mr. Vanderbilt: Please pick up line 9 for Gloria Vanderbilt. Mr. Vanderbilt: Gloria Vanderbilt: line 9". As it turned out, the one time she called — the afternoon before the morning of our flight — I was at my desk. And I was not on the phone. I knew it must be important.

"Oh Art, something terrible has happened," Gloria began in her breathless voice. I braced myself for the worst. "Scazy is going to be on our flight!"

She paused dramatically to let the impact of this sink in. "So I had to change our reservations."

She waited for my reaction.

I had no idea what she was talking about. What, or who, is a Scazy? A new airborne virus plague? A hijacker? An assassin? An international terrorist intent on blowing up planes? I had missed the *Nightly News* the evening before; I hadn't yet read the morning paper. What did I miss? I gave what I thought was an appropriately grateful "oh my gosh! Thank goodness you were able to change them!" as I madly googled Scazy.

Scazy? Skasi? Scarsi? Scarzy? Was it a moniker for someone whose face had been cut in a knife fight and was scared? I could see him: nightmarish livid white scars that cut across his cheeks. I shivered. What was she saying? I searched all sorts of combinations, coming up only with Arnold Scaasi who ran a very high-end couture salon in New York City, catering to socialites and celebrities, from Barbra Streisand to Elizabeth Taylor, to Lauren Bacall, Joan

Crawford, Brooke Astor, to a host of First Ladies, but no mention at all about any criminal or terrorist proclivities. How did you even spell it? Had I misunderstood what she had said? I wrote down the new flight information she gave me, we'd meet at the gate the next morning, 7:15 a.m. "Man we dodged that bullet," I told her as we said goodbye; "Good work!"

I consider myself punctual, some friends would say obsessively so, the rest would say neurotically so, so I arrived at the airport almost an hour before Gloria said to be there, checked my bags and got through security. As I approached our gate, I could see I was way early, there was just one person sitting there, all alone in a chair by the gate.

As always, I had to look closely to be sure. Gloria once again had disappeared in public. As usual there was nothing flashy about her attire. She never looked around. Or even looked up.

I walked over to her.

"Mrs. Vanderbilt, I presume?" I asked.

She looked. "Mr. Vanderbilt. Please, have a seat," and patted the seat next to her.

We sat and talked as the chairs in the waiting area slowly began to fill with groggy early morning travelers who had no idea who was sitting there with them.

We were deep in conversation, it was almost time to board, when I sensed my space being invaded. Someone was standing directly in front of us. Much too close. Neither of us looked up. We continued talking.

"Hello, Gloria," the person said.

Gloria looked up and, without missing a beat, said: "Hello Scaasi."

My head jerked back. I stared at him. He didn't look like a terrorist, he didn't look threatening. Was he a stalker who had been served with a restraining order to stay 1,500 feet away from Miss

Vanderbilt? He appeared to be in his late sixties, early seventies, wearing a very smart blue blazer with a colorful pocket handker- chief, a striped shirt and very expensive looking silk tie, perfectly pressed gray flannel slacks, Gucci loafers.

"You are looking very handsome this morning, Arnold," Gloria said.

Scaasi puffed up a little. "Well, you better get used to this outfit because it's all you're going to be seeing for the next few days."

He looked at me, and Gloria introduced us.

"And what do you do," he asked me. "Are you a gentleman of leisure?"

Which struck me as quite amusing, a partner at a law firm where everyone was expected to, had to, bill at least 200 hours a month; not only to physically be there for 200 hours, but to have done work that could be billed to clients, that would pay for those hours. Try that sometime. It had taken the contortions of a Laocoon to try to arrange my schedule to take a few days off. We said a few words to Scaasi and his partner, Parker Ladd, a distinguished looking gentle- man of about the same age, and then they were off into the crowd.

"I can't believe this," Gloria said. "They must have changed their flight just like I did."

Gloria told me she had learned the day before that Scaasi, who had just published a book, *Women I Have Dressed and Undressed*, would be appearing at the same event, which had led to her scram- ble and shift flights. "I'll tell you later all about him," she said with a roll of her eyes. "At least we're free of them, there will be so many people there. They are expecting thousands, they tell me."

Of course, as fate would have it, Scaasi and Parker had the seats directly across the aisle from us. So Gloria couldn't fill me in on her concern. And when we landed in Scottsdale, they stayed with us — by now we had bonded, familiar faces in a new land — as we went together to the baggage claim area.

The conveyor came around and Gloria, with one dainty pinky, lifted off her very slim, very tiny little travel case, which looked like a diplomat's attaché case which might hold — at most — ten pieces of paper. Around came the carousel again and Scaasi and Parker lifted off their similar-sized attaché cases. They all looked at me, anxious to set off in the *Town Cars* waiting for us. I was hoping they would be looking elsewhere, but all three were staring, in disbelief, when around came my large suitcase, which I had to man-handle off the conveyor belt with two hands. The three turned and started walking away.

"I have one more," I whispered, hoping there was not too much sweat dripping off my brow from lifting the suitcase.

A couple revolutions more and I grabbed at the large garment bag, which I pretended was as light as a feather.

Here I am: with one of the perennially Best Dressed Women of the World. Here I am with the World Famous Designer who dresses all the best dressed women of the world. And they are glancing back at me as if Bette Midler, Mariah Carey, Celine Dion, and Cher all rolled into one — the world's biggest diva — is following them with his hourly change of attire.

Alone at last in the *Phoenician*, registered to our delight as Mr. and Mrs. Vanderbilt, giddy at finally arriving, we were like two mischievous thirteen year olds with no parental supervision. Everything was funny, everything was fun.

Truman Capote's most famous fictional creation was Holly Golightly in *Breakfast at Tiffany's*, a character he based on Gloria, his good pal in the 1940s and 1950s. There's a scene in the novel where Holly and the narrator spend a carefree day walking around the City:

We giggled, ran, sang along the paths toward the old wooden boathouse, and then, passing a Woolworth's, she gripped my arm: "Let's steal something," she said, pulling me into the store … Holly picked up a mask and slipped it over her face; she chose another and put it on mine; then she took my hand and we walked away. It was as simple as that. Outside, we ran a few blocks, I think to make it more dramatic.

I saw in the *Phoenician* that that was vintage Gloria. And had no doubt that Gloria and Truman had done just that, and that his fictional character, Holly, captured well the Gloria he knew and I was coming to know.

The only activity that first evening was a cocktail reception and dinner in the Grand Ballroom. It was scheduled to begin at 7:00 p.m., so of course Gloria and I glamed up and found our way to be obediently there at 7:00 p.m. On the dot.

The ballroom was enormous with tables set up that easily would accommodate 1,000 guests. And not another soul was in the room. It was empty.

We looked at each other.

"Do you think we could skip this?" Gloria asked me, with the answer in her pleading eyes.

We both had arisen early to be at Newark Airport for our flight. There was a two hour time difference in Arizona, so 7:00 in the Grand Ballroom was the equivalent of 9:00 p.m. at home in our pajamas. A cocktail reception, a formal dinner for over one thousand guests, a program of speakers. This evening could easily go on for four hours. One o'clock a.m. our time — way past the bedtimes of two weary travelers. Once the crowd started to fill the room, it would be harder to escape. Gloria was one of five authors being celebrated, including Scaasi and Senator John McCain. We wouldn't be missed in the mob.

"I agree. Let's escape while we can."

As quietly as two mice, we fast walked out of the Ballroom and out of the danger zone, delighted in our cunning when at last we reached the safety of our rooms.

We called Room Service, had dinner delivered, devoured it, and retired.

It wasn't long before our phones were ringing. Our doors rapped. But like Anne Frank with her family, we hid in our own attic annex.

From the moment we awoke and emerged from our rooms, we were all but under house arrest. Two of the once lovely ladies in charge of the event were assigned to us — lovely ladies who turned into Gestapo guards — one for Gloria, one for me, her dangerous side kick, and their mission was never — never! — let us out of sight. From then on. If we had to go to the restroom, they went with us and stood right outside the door until we emerged, and walked us back to where we should be. Gloria and I looked at each other: we were trapped! This was to be our punishment for misbehaving. We looked on with envy as Scaasi wandered here and there, a free man, carefree, once coming over to us and saying under his breath, "see what happens when you misbehave?" wagging his finger at us as he strode away.

Somehow Scaasi at the book signing had managed to commandeer a table on a raised dais, and there he sat, looking out over his fawning subjects like a feudal lord, with Parker standing at attention behind his right shoulder, ready to protect his lord and master and carry out his wishes. I had bought several copies of his book to give to friends and stood in a line which, in its eerie orderliness, resembled nothing so much as the line making its way toward Seinfeld's Soup Nazi. When my turn had come and Scassi had honored me with his autograph — though he seemed a little put out that he had to sign three books, each with a different inscriptions to a different friend— I stepped aside and asked Parker if he would also sign them. I thought that would be a nice gesture since he had been so gracious and so much fun, and Scaasi's book, after all, had been dedicated to him, but at my modest proposal he looked instantly smitten and flustered. His impeccable patrician composure slipped, clearly he had never been asked to do this before, and he said he would have to ask His Majesty if it would be alright. I did not say what was on the tip of my tongue — "for god's sakes man, grow a pair!" — but stood aside as he got obediently back, at the back of the line, and patiently waited for an audience. Scassi considered this outlandish request for a moment, then rendered his verdict with an imperial wave of his hand and an exasperated "oh, alright", whereupon poor Parker signed them, with a look like he was doing something wrong, like he was defiling the Bible, and would later have to pay the inevitable penalty.

Gloria was gamely signing hundreds of books and posing for hundreds of photos. As noontime approached when she, and the other authors, would give their talks, she asked our guard if the guard would arrange for a taxi to be available right after lunch to take us to the airport.

Our guard sneered. "YOU are not going anywhere."

As if there had been some mistake, Gloria very politely explained that we had to be at the airport for a flight leaving at 2 o'clock.

The guard laughed, a cruel, cutting laugh. "YOU are not leaving until the afternoon reception is over."

Frightened and in horror Gloria stared at her, speechless. "But, but" she began, "Scaasi is leaving."

Our guard, who seemed somehow to have changed out of her St. John suit into a SS uniform, complete with armband, smirked. "We don't care what Scaasi is doing. YOU will be here" and all but gave the Nazi salute.

We cringed. We cowered. Gloria called her faithful helper in New York and after a frantic conversation whispered to me: "We're on the red eye. We'll be landing in Newark at 3:45 a.m. We have to get out of here! Today!"

And so, like the Von Trapp family singers going through the motions of their last performance in Austria before escaping over the Alps, Gloria sat down and put on her practiced smile as more guests lined up with their books and cameras.

Elated to be escaping, relieved it was over, we talked of everything on the flight home. Gloria showed me the necklace Frank Sinatra had given her which she always wore when she traveled. How she had shown it to her friend Nancy Reagan on Air Force One when they flew with the body of the President back to California. I asked her questions about her childhood I had been curious about when writing *Fortune's Children* about her recollections of The Breakers, Aunt Gertrude, her beloved nurse Dodo, whether she still had her father's horse racing trophies, details of Truman Capote's Black and White Ball. I worked up the courage to ask her how it had been to have sex with Marlon Brando when she was thirty and he had just filmed *On the Waterfront*. "When you feel that way about someone," she said with a distant gaze, "how could it be anything but magical?"

She told me her Scassi story — how he had seen her at a party and invited her to his atelier, where — I could picture it — like a little girl she tried on fabulous gown after gown and raved about each, how a box of them arrived by messenger the next day. Along with Scassi's invoice of close to $100,000. How Gloria had back pedaled out of that one by having the box returned to him along with her gracious note that there had been a terrible mistake. She had avoided him ever since then.

Arriving in Newark in the wee hours of the morning to a deserted terminal, grungy, exhausted, we found our drivers and said goodbye.

My phone rang at 7:00 a.m. It was Gloria calling to see how I had slept, to laugh about our adventures with the lovely Nazi guards, and to tell me about the next book she wanted to write.

There would be more in the months and years ahead, more plans, more books, more fun, much more laughter.

Gloria invited me to be her guest at a dinner party at Joyce Carol Oates' home in Princeton. Like me, Joyce was another example of Gloria's philosophy in action, that "The phone can ring and your whole life can change ... Today may even be the day you meet someone who will change your life." Gloria had been moved by a poem Joyce had published in *The New Yorker*, and wrote her a fan letter to which Joyce replied, which started an abiding friendship between the two.

I arrived way too early and drove around the neighborhood for a while, trying to keep up my courage. At last, I knocked on the door and Joyce's husband, Raymond Smith, answered. Here I was, the first one there, a stranger, holding a big bouquet of tulips, praying Gloria would arrive any minute and save me. But saving was not necessary, for Ray and Joyce were immediately welcoming and gracious and non-threatening and showed me around their home deep in the woods, the portrait of them Gloria had painted, several of Gloria's Dream Box creations. If ever there was a modern-day salon it was here, in the home of these quiet unassuming friends, and at this party, and others to come, I met Edmund White and Seward Johnson, Paul Krugman, a dazzling array of Princeton professors. On the couch, talking to someone, I stared at a man crossing the room who looked so familiar; he mouthed "hi" and walked over to the bar area. "Steve Martin" my couch partner whispered. "He and Joyce share a passion for art."

Gloria and I would leave together that evening after dinner, and I would walk out with her to make sure she would find her driver in the dark. "Baboo, Baboo" she would call out in a tiny voice that no one a few steps from us would even hear, — "Baboo" — but he always instantly appeared. I followed their car along the dark winding country roads out to Route 206 to make sure I would find my way home. "Wherever you're going, I'm going your way."

Thank you, Gloria. Holly. My Huckleberry friend. To be with

you was to experience exactly what you had spoken about in your lunch talk in Scottsdale.

"The miracle to be reborn with each day, the miracle of each night to descend into the darkness of dreams and wake into the new day. It may be the day you fall in love with a tree, a flower, a face you see passing by in a taxi, a change in the weather. It's the miracle of the hour as day turns into night, and you turn on the radio and unexpectedly hear a song that brings back a memory of happiness so clearly that you are right back there when it happened. It may be the smell of bread baking, or a cake of soap as you unwrap it. Today may even be the day you meet someone who will change your life …"

ABOUT THE AUTHOR

 A graduate of Wesleyan University and the University of Virginia School of Law, Arthur T. Vanderbilt II is the author of many books of history, biography, memoirs and essays. His books have been selections of the Book-of-the-Month Club, *Reader's Digest*'s "Today's Best Nonfiction," the Easton Press Series of the 100 Best Books of American History, and other book clubs, and have been serialized in newspapers and magazines, translated into foreign languages, excerpted in anthologies, and optioned for television and film. He lives in New Jersey.

Made in United States
North Haven, CT
28 May 2022

19612998R00090